# ECO-
# VISION
# ARIES

# ECO-VISIONARIES

**ART, ARCHITECTURE, AND NEW MEDIA AFTER THE ANTHROPOCENE**

HATJE CANTZ

# CONTENT

**07      PEDRO GADANHO**

**13      SABINE HIMMELSBACH**

**17      KARIN OHLENSCHLÄGER**

**21      KATARINA PIERRE**

**25      ESSAYS AND WORKS**

**34      LINDA WEINTRAUB**
VISIONARY ECO-ART: NEXT/NOW/PAST

**52      AMALE ANDRAOS**
THE TIMELINESS OF ARCHITECTURE'S ECO-VISIONARY PRACTICES

**72      MARIANA PESTANA**
ECO-VISIONARIES: ART AND ARCHITECTURE AFTER
THE ANTHROPOCENE

**92      SOFIA JOHANSSON**
OUR PLACE ON EARTH

**110     YVONNE VOLKART**
ECODATA—ECOMEDIA—ECO-AESTHETICS: TECHNOLOGIES OF THE
ECOLOGICAL AFTER THE ANTHROPOCENE

**130     MATTHEW FULLER**
FIGURING ECOLOGIES

**148     T. J. DEMOS**
THE ARTS OF LIVING AT THE END OF THE WORLD

**170     LIST OF WORKS**

# THE ENDLESS SUMMER

Are we just secretly yearning for an endless summer? Perhaps. Imagine a constant, moderately hot climate when we have harnessed, and now endlessly enjoy, the energy of sun, waves, and wind. Never mind winter sports, or hell in Cambodia. Imagine a whole continent modeled on the permanent California dream. Forget the wild fires, or growing homeless populations. Imagine the tropical renaissance of Southern Europe, and the ever-better quality of life of winterless Northern Europe. Ignore the severe drought outside tourist-ridden cities, or a few crazy storms like they used to have in the Caribbean. Picture ever-fizzling burgers by a luscious, constantly recreated, J.G. Ballard-like seaside. Dismiss what was once the Netherlands, or the wind turbine-crowned offshore walls restraining climate refugees. Envisage the perpetual holidays provided by artificial intelligence and a few massive twists of geo-engineering. Disregard the unexpected consequences of more fiddling with the planet's surface. Visualize a pleasant, fully operational, Internet of things-driven endless summer. Never mind that it is just for a few of us. You win some, you lose some. Are we to blame if we secretly wish for a technologically ensured, corporately maintained endless summer?

The endless summer is a seminal surf movie, a 1994 Donna Summer compilation, a genetically modified tomato, a total of 2,940,000 hits on YouTube, and a 2005 episode of *SpongeBob SquarePants* on the effects of global warming[1]—reminding us of how the unconscious of children and teenagers is now fed on brutal issues through TV series and franchise movies. Think Pixar's *Wall-E* for the effects of overconsumption, waste, pollution, the sixth extinction, and an endless summer looking for a new planet to inhabit. More tellingly, "The Endless Summer" is also one of the first mainstream essays on the *greenhouse effect,* published thirty years ago in *Discover* magazine.[2] What has happened since NASA's James Hansen first alerted the US Senate to *global warming?* Terminology has evolved, and we now feel the multiple torching effects of *climate change.* And yet, climate change denial is on the rise. By March 2017, the *Politico* website reported how Twitter-President Donald Trump's Department of Energy forbade the use of the term.[3] A talk show host snappily suggested using the expression "endless summer" instead. Perhaps uncomfortable facts would then disappear.

As scientists, philosophers, and others have noted, one of the greatest difficulties in dealing with climate change resides in the ability to effectively communicate its phenomena and effects to a non-specialist audience. Information is readily available. The subject has been widely covered in the media. People are in fact bombarded with partial evidence of climate change on a daily basis. And yet, climate change, and its widespread ecological consequences, does not seem to *register* in people's minds. When researching last summer, I confronted what appeared to be my own ignorance on the theme—only to realize that I had already come across most of the information, and had readily forgotten it. Over the years, I had read about greenhouse and carbon-burning effects, multi-species extinctions, weather disruptions, ocean acidification, extreme forms of pollution, environmental poisoning.

Naturally, I had come across the array of disastrous impacts of human activity on the surface of the planet, which is now trendily aggregated under the geological label of "the Anthropocene." However, as with practically everybody else, I had encountered these phenomena as fragments scattered in several reports and news pieces. I had never confronted the isolated evidence—and the reflections upon it—as a part of one overall, massive phenomenon. Out of this dispersion—and out of a very human, psychological need to postpone the signs of coming disaster—I, as anybody else, tended to dismiss the subject's darker dimension.

The idea of *Eco-Visionaries* as a multi-partner, curatorial endeavour arose precisely as an attempt at a more complex, overarching, and yet audience-driven take on the diversity of issues surrounding today's ecological global transformations. Art, architecture, and new media practices have increasingly reflected on diverse aspects and outcomes of human-induced planetary change. Yet, the expression of this interest in the exhibition realm has been mostly narrowly themed, and again fragmented in nature. The collaborative publication that you hold in your hands, as well as the independent shows appearing over the span of one year at MAAT, Bildmuseet, HeK, and LABoral, offers, by contrast, a broad and up-to-date view by juxtaposing four different curatorial perspectives. Thus, we envisioned connecting the views that have emerged from ecological art to architects' investigations into the depletion of resources, or to interactive designers' imagined adaptations to a new reality, but also to how media artists are delving into big data to offer much needed critical perspectives on the perceived state of the planet's distressed ecosystem.

Together with the new essays published here, the glimpses into the multiplicity of points of view gathered in *Eco-Visionaries* give you a broader picture of the incremental, interrelated aspects of the climate and ecological changes affecting us today. The project started from the optimistic premise that we need alternative visions of the future if indeed we want to face up to such changes. Our research revealed much more pessimistic scenarios, and the need to also embrace critical visions that may lay bare what often remains hidden. As Linda Weintraub unveils here when she probes into the history of eco-art's pioneers, this duality has been present since the sixties. Yet, it is surely no coincidence that, even if not tagged as ecologists, more artists and architects have recently felt the need to share their investigations into the overwhelming issues of ecological change. Why? As a *New York Times* columnist put it back in 2012, "the climate has changed, and the only remaining questions may well be: a) how bad will things get, and b) how long will it be before we wake up to it."[4] Perhaps it is finally the time when more people need to wake up to it. Perhaps it is finally a question of survival that more people absorb, remember, and act upon the multiple impacts of the endless summer we are entering.

*PEDRO GADANHO*
DIRECTOR, MAAT—MUSEU DE ARTE, ARQUITETURA E TECNOLOGIA

---

1   It is perhaps no coincidence that *SpongeBob SquarePants* is created by a marine biologist, Stephen Hillenburg.

2   As reported in a landmark statement from June 23, 1988: "James Hansen of the NASA Goddard Institute for Space Studies testified before a Senate committee that he could state with '99 percent confidence' that a recent, persistent rise in global temperature was occurring, and had long been expected." See Andrew C. Revkin, "Special Report: Endless Summer—Living with the Greenhouse Effect," *Discover* (June 23, 2008), http://discovermagazine.com/1988/oct/23-special-report-endless-summer-living-with-the-greenhouse-effect (accessed December, 2017).

3   See Eric Wolff, "Energy Department Climate Office Bans Use of Phrase 'Climate Change,'" *Politico*, 29 March, 2017, https://www.politico.com/story/2017/03/energy-department-climate-change-phrases-banned-236655 (accessed December, 2017).

4   As Mark Bittman concluded at the time, "the only sane people who don't see this as a problem are those whose profitability depends on the status quo." See "The Endless Summer," *The New York Times,* July 18, 2012, https://opinionator.blogs.nytimes.com/2012/07/18/the-endless-summer/ (accessed December, 2017).

# WE ARE CONFRONTED

nearly every day with dramatic images of extreme weather phenomena—of hurricanes, flooding, or forest fires due to extreme drought. The first decade of the twenty-first century was the warmest decade in a long time. It has meanwhile been factually proven that global warming is advancing, ocean temperatures are rising, glaciers are melting, permafrost regions are shrinking, and the ice sheets at the poles are disappearing. Political action has nonetheless been halting, and the measures agreed on in the Paris climate agreement in 2015 in order to achieve the climate-protection objectives that were set are insufficient. In 2017, the United States even threatened to withdraw from the global agreement in 2020. At the same time, it has also been factually proven that global warming is largely caused by human beings, and that human beings have become one of the most important factors influencing biological, geological, and atmospheric processes on the earth.

The exhibition *Ecomedia*[1] in 2007 was already dedicated to the phenomena described, with a focus on ecology and sustainability. Based on the artistic projects presented at the time, the exhibition demonstrated not only that the natural catastrophes described are not "natural," but also that they are uncontrollable effects of highly civilized and dominant living beings—something that is currently denoted with the term Anthropocene as a new geo-chronological epoch. *Ecomedia* regarded ecology and sustainability as a communication system in which the relevant actors—from human beings and animals to organic and inorganic substances—are in constant exchange and interaction.

Ten years after this exhibition, it seemed to the curators that it was time to shed fresh light on the topic from a current perspective, and to once again examine the role of art with respect to an artistic practice that is interlinked with media and reflects the influence of media technologies in a discourse with science, technology, and eco-activism. Current developments in the direction of the Anthropocene, geo-media, and earth media clearly show that the then rather speculatively expressed theory of eco-media has become even more relevant—this is one reason why the title from 2007 has once again been taken up in the curatorial statement with the terms "eco-data—eco-media—eco-aesthetics," so as to inquire into shifts, among other things, from a time distance of ten years.

The HeK is dedicated to digital culture and the new art forms of the information age. It is a venue for critical discourse on the aesthetic, sociopolitical, and economic effects of media technologies. In this sense, the exhibition focuses on new media, technologies, and techno-scientific methods in the arts and on their significance for the perception and awareness of the "ecological." As a result, the materiality of the earth is observed and assessed above all in its interpretation as data. The exhibition inquires into the ways, means, and possibilities of producing techno-aesthetic relationships to our environment. It sensitizes visitors to the urgent ecological problems and questions of our time and attempts to show sustainable creative possibilities.

SABINE HIMMELSBACH
DIRECTOR, HEK—HAUS DER ELEKTRONISCHEN KÜNSTE BASEL

---

1   The exhibition *Ecomedia* was curated by Sabine Himmelsbach, Karin Ohlenschläger, and Yvonne Volkart for the Edith-Russ-Haus for Media Art in Oldenburg. It was subsequently also presented at Plug.in, the institution that preceded the HeK. Further information about the exhibition can be found in the catalogue of the same name: Sabine Himmelsbach and Yvonne Volkart, eds., *Ecomedia: Ecological Strategies in Today's Art* (Ostfildern, 2007).

**WE HAVE BEEN AWARE** of the consequences of industrial development for the environment since, at the latest, Rachel Carson's book *Silent Spring* (1962). At the time, her work involved above all the use of pesticides and the need to protect the earth from the unsustainable activities of humankind—the *animal* whose collective thinking and action initiated the age of the noosphere:[1] an epoch in which human beings' collective intelligence would change the surface of the earth just as biological and geological forces had done in the past.

Despite the knowledge of the causes of current environmental problems that has been gathered in recent decades, development has so far barely changed.[2] In the meantime, as part of the global ecosystem, not only plants and animals but also human beings remain at risk. This is substantiated by recent studies.[3] Pollutants in the air, water, and ground alone are responsible for nine million premature deaths per year worldwide. That equals *three times more deaths than those due to AIDS, tuberculosis, and malaria together, and fifteen times more than all wars and other forms of violence.*

In her book, Rachel Carlson demonstrated how art and culture can positively contribute to this complex problem through linking scientific environmental data and people's personal experiences, and hence also enable a broader public to understand abstract knowledge.

In doing so, she rendered a fact visible that is important today, namely, that it is not only factual knowledge that is decisive in increasing the awareness of the environment; an impetus for new thinking and action is also provided by direct, empathetic experience, and by making it possible—in the double sense of the word—to grasp problems.

In the past few decades, the art world has taken on precisely this task. In dialogue with science, technology, and society, art has shown, for one thing, that environmental issues are subject to ever-greater global complexity and systems thinking. For this reason, among others, artists today are increasingly working in a transdisciplinary way on projects in which nature and technology, experience and knowledge, facts and feelings, and ethics and aesthetics are interlinked anew.

In this context, it has been important to the LABoral art center for many years to promote dialogue and transdisciplinary collaboration; to link education, research, production, and exhibitions in new, open structures and make them more dynamic. This also means supporting projects in which ideas and visions, along with action-related engagement on the part of art, science, and technology, provide an impetus for changing our social, political, and economic behavior.

With this aim in mind, it is of particular importance for us to be able to address such an urgent and complex topic of our time—environmental issues and the Anthropocene—in cooperation with Bildmuseet in Umeå, HeK in Basel, and MAAT in Lisbon. We are deeply thankful to all of our partners and curators for this collaboration.

*KARIN OHLENSCHLÄGER*
*ARTISTIC DIRECTOR, LABORAL CENTRO DE ARTE Y CREACIÓN INDUSTRIAL*

1   This term was coined in the "detheologized" form above all by Vladimir I. Vernadsky. See "The Biosphere and the Noosphere," *American Scientist* 33, no. 1 (1945), pp. 1–12.

2   William J. Ripple et al., "World Scientists' Warning to Humanity: A Second Notice," *BioScience* 67, no. 12 (December, 2017), pp. 1026–28, https://academic.oup.com/bioscience/article/67/12/1026/4605229 (accessed November, 2017).

3   Philip J. Landrigan et al., "The Lancet Commission on Pollution and Health," *The Lancet* 391, no. 10,119 (February, 2018), http://www.thelancet.com/journals/lancet/article/PIIS0140-6736(17)32345-0/fulltext (accessed November, 2017).

# THE WINTERS IN

Umeå are becoming milder. Instead of sparkling snow we have rain, and instead of clear, cold winter days, with the sun shining from a blue sky, we have gray mist and heavy clouds. The sea does not freeze over as it used to do, and the reindeers in northern Sweden have to be emergency fed because the snow has been replaced by ice, which prevents them from reaching the lichen. Other parts of the world are beset by extreme weather, droughts, floods, and hurricanes… The glaciers are melting and the oceans are rising. The world is changing and we do not know what to do, what we can do.

Many of the artists we have presented at Bildmuseet in recent years have addressed the issue of our responsibility for the environment, nature, and climate. The indelible marks we leave behind in the water, the air, and the earth were a common theme in the exhibition *Perpetual Uncertainty: Contemporary Art in the Nuclear Anthropocene.* Biological diversity, land exploitation, and the fight for the earth's resources were themes in *The Sovereign Forest* by Amar Kanwar, Sudhir Pattnaik, and Sherna Dastur. Our dark and painful relationship with the sea throughout history was addressed by John Akomfrah in the video installation *Vertigo Sea,* and in his new work, *Purple,* we encounter ourselves in our vulnerable and at the same time autocratic position in the human era, the Anthropocene.

The exhibition *Eco-Visionaries* at Bildmuseet presents artists whose work can inspire our thoughts and actions, works that insist that other mental, social, and economic ecologies are possible. I would like to extend my heartfelt thanks to the participating artists for sharing their ideas and experiences. I would also like to thank Pedro Gadanho at MAAT for inviting us to participate in this stimulating project. The opportunity to collaborate and discuss this theme with international colleagues at other art institutions has been greatly rewarding. Thanks also to Sofia Johansson, the curator at Bildmuseet who successfully curated and project-managed *Eco-Visionaries*. And thanks to all our co-workers at Bildmuseet who have helped make possible this important exhibition.

In conjunction with *Eco-Visionaries,* at Bildmuseet we offer a comprehensive program of lectures, guided tours, and workshops. In addition to the exhibition's artists, a number of researchers from Umeå University will share their knowledge and expertise. Bildmuseet is part of Umeå University and this closeness to scientific research and current debate enables us to create thought-provoking encounters between disciplines, times, and places.

KATARINA PIERRE
DIRECTOR, BILDMUSEET, UMEÅ UNIVERSITY

# ESSAYS AND WORKS

Basim Magdy, *Our Prehistoric Fate*, 2011

Semiconductor, *Earthworks*, 2016

Wanuri Kahiu, *Pumzi,* 2009, video still

Andrés Jaque, *Island House in Laguna Grande, Corpus Christi, Texas*, 2015–ongoing

# VISIONARY ECO-ART: NEXT/ NOW/ PAST

*LINDA WEINTRAUB*

### INTRODUCTION

Artworks from across time and space provide evidence that "nature" once inspired wonder, epitomized beauty, embodied wisdom, instilled reverence, and revealed God's glory. People's relationship with the special planet they inhabit shifted in the 1970s as evidence mounted that human activities were jeopardizing Earth's biological, meteorological, and geological assets. Throughout this era, smog, pollution, DDT poisoning, industrial waste, famine, atomic fallout, and oil spills grew into an alarming litany of environmental afflictions.

Artists who were "first responders" to impending planetary crises confronted the challenge of integrating into the arena of art the guilt and fear that had encroached upon human relationships with nonhuman realms. The pioneering strategies and processes they introduced into their art practices are now acknowledged as inaugurating today's eco-art movement. Indeed, their explorations were so exceptional that they earned the adjective "visionary."

Haus-Rucker-Co, *Environment Transformer*, 1968

"Visionary art" is frequently defined as art that transcends the physical world to evoke mystical realities. Alex Grey (b. 1953), a leading visionary artist, explains, "Our scientific, materialist culture trains us to develop the eyes of outer perception. Visionary art encourages the development of our inner sight. To find the visionary realm, we use the intuitive inner eye: the eye of contemplation; the eye of the soul."[1]

"Visionary eco-art," in contrast, is rooted in the material substances and entities that comprise the ecosystems of the planet. Because ecology explores events that register in the physical world and carry functional consequences, the definition of the word "visionary" that applies to this exhibition and publication asserts that eco-visionary artists envision tangible and measurable conditions of Earth systems. Eco-art visionaries might ask:

Will remediation initiatives succeed?
Will global temperatures stabilize?
Will humans prevail?

In seeking answers to such questions, eco-visionaries may be pragmatists or romanticists, resisters or conformists, social theorists or natural scientists, rights of nature advocates or social reformers. This essay explores an archetypal dyad—optimists and pessimists. While contrast provides this essay's organizing scheme, it is the impetus to address the sobering evidence of environmental blights it sheds that enriches this discussion. Because an afflicted planet seems more pitiful than inspiring, in the past both groups of artists suspended the tradition of "taking" inspiration from nature. Optimists "offered" ways to restore Earth's material splendor. Pessimists "conceded" its depleted state.

These twentieth-century responses to environmental degradation still prevail in the twenty-first century, but they lack the revolutionary zeal that originally inspired them. During the raucous counter-culture era, defenses of our beleaguered planet existed alongside denunciations of material affluence, stultifying work, commercialism, patriarchal power, military aggression, sexual restraint, and so forth.

During the decades-long hiatus between past and current eco-art movements, counter-culture exuberance was replaced with sober assessments of mounting planetary afflictions. Today, the visionary task occupying contemporary eco-artists involves anticipating the consequences of humanity's indiscretions. Optimists make determined efforts to remediate and educate. Pessimists dwell on dismal accountings and critical odds. While both groups infuse the imagination with predictions of human destiny, bypassing "now" to anticipate "next," the temporal thrust of this essay is "former." It presents two of the many pioneering eco-artist visionaries from the 1970s whose nascent innovations anticipated the sprawling creative venturing of eco-artists today.

## PESSIMIST: ROBERT SMITHSON—
## ENTROPY AND COLLAPSE

Fictionalized eco-disasters began infiltrating popular entertainment in the 1970s. Films such as *No Blade of Grass* (1970), *Silent Running* (1972), and *Soylent Green* (1973) dramatized dismal scenarios for life on Earth that seemed possible, and even probable, as news reports implicated human abuse and neglect in climate change, mass extinction, nitrogen deposition, rainforest collapse, overgrazing, acidified oceans, polluted waterways, smog-laden air, and dead lakes. These acts of "ecocide" were associated with ominous predictions of an "ecopalypse."

Robert Smithson, *Partially Buried Woodshed*, 1970

Such grave ecosystem disruptions are apparent in vast swaths of soils laced with nasty concoctions of sewage, pesticides, herbicides, industrial effluents, medical waste, spilled oil, and chemical substances, or these are sealed beneath pavement. Robert Smithson (1938–73), a prominent first-generation eco-artist, introduced soil's plight into his work by selecting asphalt as his artistic medium. This substance, mixed with gravel, is useful for paving precisely because it suppresses soil's ecological role in maintaining life on the planet. Smithson abandoned the studio and ventured outdoors to create an "earthwork" that intentionally stifled soil's life-enhancing functions. The site he selected was a gravel quarry that had become deeply scarred by open-pit mining. A sterile moonscape had resulted from the removal of soil and vegetation to gain access to valuable mineral deposits.

To create *Asphalt Rundown* (1969), Smithson confirmed the site's industrial operations by choosing a dump truck as his artistic tool, gravity as his artistic process, and hot asphalt as his artistic medium. His radical artistic process involved backing the truck to the edge of a steep bank that had eroded in the aftermath of mining excavations. Poised in this precarious position, the truck raised its bed and released an entire load of steaming hot asphalt to flow down the bank, cool, and harden. Through this action, Smithson mischievously returned the mined gravel to its point of origin. The ludicrous act of paving the mining site manifested what he called a "Humpty Dumpty way of doing things."[2] The phrase conveys the futility of reclaiming sites of industrial mining operations. Smithson explains, "You can imagine the result when they try to deal with the Bingham pit in Utah which is a pit one mile deep and three miles across…. it would take something like 30 years and they'd have to get the dirt from another mountain…. It seems that one would have to recognize this entropic condition rather than try to reverse it."[3]

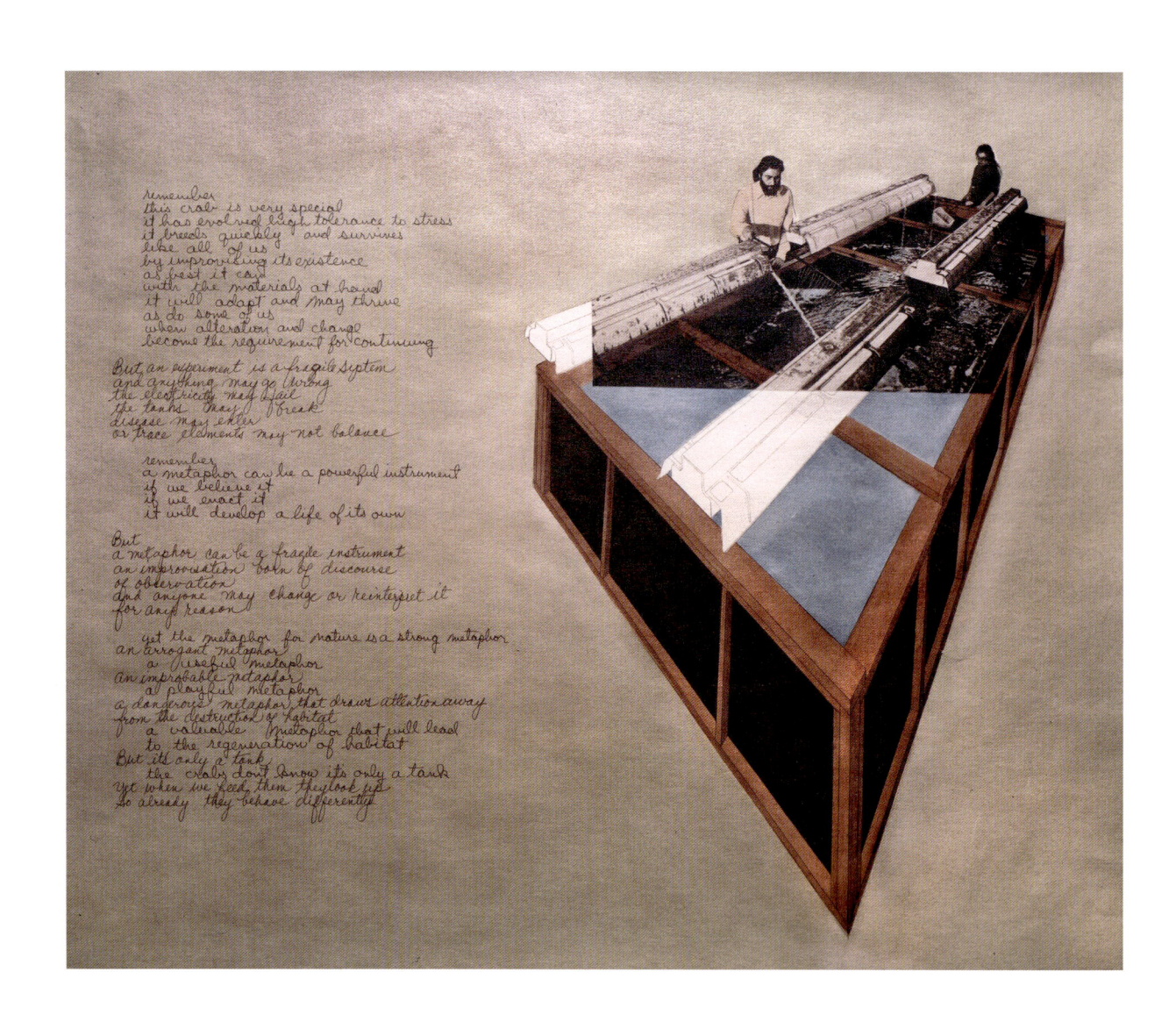

remember
   this crab is very special
   it has evolved high tolerance to stress
   it breeds quickly and survives
   like all of us
   by improvising its existence
   as best it can
   with the materials at hand
   it will adapt and may thrive
   as do some of us
   when alteration and change
   become the requirement for continuing

But an experiment is a fragile system
and anything may go wrong
   the electricity may fail
   the tanks may break
   disease may enter
   or trace elements may not balance

   remember
      a metaphor can be a powerful instrument
      if we believe it
      if we enact it
      it will develop a life of its own

But
a metaphor can be a fragile instrument
an improvisation born of discourse
of observation
and anyone may change or reinterpret it
for any reason

      yet the metaphor for nature is a strong metaphor
an arrogant metaphor
      a useful metaphor
an improbable metaphor
      a playful metaphor
a dangerous metaphor that draws attention away
from the destruction of habitat
      a valuable metaphor that will lead
         to the regeneration of habitat
But it's only a tank
      the crabs don't know it's only a tank
yet when we feed them they look up
so already they behave differently

The Harrison Studio, *The Second Lagoon—Sea Grant, The Lagoon Cycle*, 1973–84

In addition to exposing environmental threats, Smithson actualized the collapse these threats portended in a work entitled *Partially Buried Woodshed,* created at Kent State University in 1970. Because demolition was his intended outcome, he enlisted a backhoe to dump dirt on an unused shed on the campus until the supporting beam cracked and the shed collapsed. It took twenty loads of earth to raze the small structure. Although Smithson intended to leave the collapsed shed to further deteriorate in the elements, university officials removed the unsightly ruin. Nonetheless, the work offers a vivid example of the inevitable collapse that grips the minds of pessimists. Smithson reversed the cherished art tradition in which artists create something new—by demolishing something old. The principle underlying this act is derived from physics and is known as "entropy." It asserts that matter and energy are degraded or depleted during every mechanical process and material transformation. According to the law of entropy, order can only be restored with new inputs of energy. Smithson explains, "You have a closed system which eventually deteriorates and starts to break apart and there's no way that you can really piece it back together again."[4]

Entropy encapsulates the pessimist's approach to energy (energy is useless), information theory (information is lost), cosmology (matter collapses into black holes), history (eras decline into disorder), economics (material and energy degrade during production), and biology (organisms decline and die). Entropy weighs heavily on environmentalists because, by demonstrating that machines cannot create the resources they transform, it proves that resource depletion is inevitable.

*Partially Buried Woodshed* manifested the law of entropy because the creative act resulted in collapse. Nonetheless, this law is not inherently pessimistic. In vital ecosystems, entropy is paired with the complementary action that harvests energy to create order. By disassociating entropy from the cycling of energy and matter that accounts for the persistence of life on Earth, Smithson excludes the means by which ecosystems replenish the energy they lost. In the artworks presented, Smithson confronts the public with two unsettling realizations. One is the evidence of humanity's aggressive incursions on landscapes through industrial technologies. The other is the inevitability of collapse. The former tempers the euphoria surrounding material abundance. The latter undermines the confidence in systems' abilities to withstand stress. These artworks anticipate "ecocide" and the "ecopalypse."

Smithson never declared his outdoor art interventions "complete." Instead of attempting to compose a work of art that embodied his artistic vision, he introduced the radical concept of inviting surrounding forces to shape the physical state of his artworks. Welcoming changes that can neither be controlled nor anticipated has been widely accepted by contemporary eco-artists, who integrate their creative interventions into ecosystem dynamics where change is an abiding condition.

Furthermore, by identifying art as a morphing process, Smithson helped shift it away from its embodiment in an object with a constructed form. He explains, "I'm reversing the perspective to get another viewpoint, because we've seen it so long now from the decorative design point of view and not from the point of view of the physicality of the terrain."[5] Focusing on "the physicality of the terrain" meant art processes were not conducted in studios, the artwork was not a product of the artist's manual skill, and the creative act was not embodied in a commodity—meaning it was not conveyed by stylistic alterations; formalism was no longer a fundamental component. This alternative involves eliminating "representation" and presenting materials as they exist in the physical world. In this manner, medium, site, and process convey the artwork's theme.

## OPTIMISTS: HELEN MAYER HARRISON AND NEWTON HARRISON— CULTIVATION/ADAPTATION

"Try to imagine ... Earth is being wrecked globally, we are in 1968 or 1969. What's Earth? It's where everything grows.... That's when we started to think like farmers."[6] At the time Newton and Helen Mayer Harrison made this declaration, Helen Mayer Harrison had earned a master's in educational psychology and had studied literature and anthropology. Newton Harrison was a painter and sculptor. The merging of their complementary backgrounds resulted in a lifelong collaboration that originated, and then developed, many foundational principles of eco-art. "Thinking like farmers" lies at the core of their visionary innovations.

Farmers trust that seeds will germinate, sprouts will mature, fruit will ripen, and crops will thrive. Optimism is embedded in their faith in productivity. By definition, farmers cannot be cynics or pessimists. The Harrisons activated farmers' optimism throughout their fifty-year career by originating pragmatic solutions to current and impending environmental crises. Since they presented these visionary schemes within the context of an art practice, their pioneering environmental strategies also helped forge the eco-art movement, and particularly art's venture into bio-art. The Harrisons introduced living entities as art mediums, and conducted life functions as studio art practices within the context of problem solving. Their ingenious strategies continue to resonate among today's environmentalists, ecologists, and eco-artists.

The Harrisons' stalwart commitment to optimism was undeterred by mounting evidence that ecosystem disruptions were so dire that they were undermining the planet's ability to support life. The artists maintained confidence that the grand schemes they developed could reverse this doomed course and assure humanity's survival. Their whole-planet, real-time eco-art expedition was launched in 1972 when the artists traveled to Sri Lanka to study the *Scylla serrata,* a cannibal crab that survives in the dense muck of Sri Lankan lagoons.

In Sri Lanka, the crab was valued as a nutritious food and a lucrative export. To the artists, however, the crab offered the possibility of averting a food crisis if ecosystems became too corrupted, or if the climate became too unstable to yield reliable crops. Besides delighting people with its delicious taste, this special crab epitomizes strategies of survival. It possesses the uncanny ability to thrive in salty, fresh, and dirty water, regenerate damaged limbs, breed and grow quickly, stay alive out of water, tolerate wide-ranging temperatures, and digest a diverse diet. The artists noted particularly that the crab adapted to extreme conditions like those that existed when primeval life first emerged on Earth. Thus, the Harrisons conducted art as an experiment to see if this highly adaptable crab could be bred by "farmers," and if such breeding could succeed in polluted waters, like those in the Salton Sea in California, where extreme salinity and pollution have devastated fish populations. For all these reasons, the crab was studied as a model of survival skills that could be adopted by humans. The artists note, "Like all of us, [the crab] must improvise its existence very creatively with the materials at hand, but the materials keep changing."[7] Crabs are more adept at survival accommodations than humans.

The Harrisons relayed this ambitious agenda by creating an 8-foot-tall, 360-foot-long mural replete with hand-colored photographs, drawings, lists of facts, satellite images, and visionary maps that, for example, depicted future coastlines if polar ice melted. This monumental artwork also included a text of an extended, semi-autobiographical dialogue between two characters: a "Lagoon Maker" (Newton) who assumes the perspective of a builder and technician, and a "Witness" (Helen) who is reflective and cautious.

This visual/verbal artwork relays details of the artists' crab-raising experiments in their Pepper Canyon laboratory at the University of California, San Diego. The crabs they raised were imported from Sri Lanka and placed in special tanks designed to replicate conditions that tested the crabs' ability to survive. Filters replicated the cleansing of waters by tides, hoses re-created monsoons, and heaters replaced the sun. The artists' optimism emerges out of the contrasting attitudes regarding these experiments that appear in the mural as a dialogue between the Witness and the Lagoon Maker. When the Witness frets that artificial lagoons are not "self-nourishing self-cleansing self-adjusting"[8] like real lagoons, she provides an opportunity for the Lagoon Maker to offer an optimistic solution: "Then suppose we adapt ourselves to supply what the crab needs … the system becomes self-nourishing self-cleansing self-adjusting then the metaphor for nature becomes more complete and we cannot represent this system without representing ourselves."[9] His tactic was enacted by the artists, who continually revised their care-giving regimens to replicate the annual gyrations in Sri Lankan lagoon conditions.

The Lagoon Maker's optimistic anticipations were fulfilled! The crabs did survive and mate in the artificial conditions they were provided. This accomplishment not only pioneered a new application of artistic creativity in which artists partnered with a nonhuman life form, it also pioneered a new application of aquatic farming that was recognized by the scientific community. This triumphant narrative appears in the *Lagoon Cycle* artwork in the section titled *Sea Grants*. The title announces that the experiment was so significant it was awarded a grant from the National Sea Grant College Program, which is run by the National Oceanic and Atmospheric Administration within the US Department of Commerce. Newton comments, "It was our first actual work that blended provable experimental science into a work of art."[10]

With the statement "We want to give life back to dead parts of the earth. Salvation depends on compliance with inherent systems,"[11] the Harrisons demonstrated that technology could be detached from dominance and exploitation, and reformulated to support natural systems. Replacing assertiveness with responsiveness is one of the defining characteristics of contemporary eco-art that can be traced to the Harrisons' pioneering initiatives. Other enduring innovations include creating art to benefit nonhuman populations; merging art, science, and ecology; and introducing into art patterns that originate in energy flows and material cycles, instead of the artist's imagination.

The functionality of the Harrisons' innovations has been adopted by many eco-artists who ignore the presumption that art's intrinsic value is corrupted by utility. Instead of raising crabs, these artists reject art-for-art's sake mandates by designing urban storm water catchments, soil remediation strategies, and energy production schemes, for example. The functional applications of their creative enterprises incorporate empirical evidence and technical expertise into the artist's skill set.

## CONCLUSION

The history of civilization is a narrative of yearning and striving. The contemporary era may be the first time in all of human history when abundance and luxury are not confined to stories that involve magic cauldrons and mysterious horns of plenty. However, the results of actualized abundance for ordinary people may surprise previous generations. It suggests that while human minds and bodies are not well served by want, they are also taxed by profusion. This is because many of the technological and scientific achievements responsible for fulfilling the material fantasies of our ancestors are responsible for jeopardizing our existence.

Eco-artists of all persuasions seek a proper niche for humans among millions of species that share the Earth's resources. Our fate might be determined by their respective assessments of "success" and "progress." Pessimists evoke despair. Optimists evoke hope. While this essay focuses on historic eco-art explorations, it concludes with the appeal to everyone to help construct a springboard into a resilient future.

---

1   Alex Grey, "What is Visionary Art?" www.alexgrey.com, last modified February 16, 2018, http://www.alexgrey.com/media/writing/essays/what-is-visionary-art/ (accessed October, 2017).

2   Robert Smithson, interview by Alison Sky, "Entropy Made Visible," *On Site* 4 (1973).

3   Ibid.

4   Ibid.

5   Robert Smithson, "Fragments of a Conversation," ed. William C. Lipke, *robertsmithson.com,* 2001, http://www.robertsmithson.com/essays/fragments.htm (accessed October, 2017).

6   Helen Mayer Harrison and Newton Harrison, "Helen and Newton Harrison in Conversation with Brandon Ballengee," in *Transdiscourse 1: Mediated Environments,* ed. Andrea Gleiniger et al. (Vienna, 2010), p. 47.

7   Helen Mayer Harrison and Newton Harrison, *The Lagoon Cycle* (Ithaca, 1985), p. 60.

8   Ibid., p. 44.

9   Ibid.

10  Newton Harrison, interview by the author, November 11, 2017.

11  Helen Mayer Harrison and Newton Harrison, "Notes on a Recent Project," *Los Angeles Institute of Contemporary Art* 16 (October–November, 1977), p. 28. Reproduced in Helen Mayer Harrison and Newton Harrison, *The Lagoon Cycle* (Ithaca, 1985), p. 20.

Krištof Kintera, *Postnaturalia Herbario Plate*, 2016

Wasted Rita, *The Future Is Written*, 2016

THE FUTURE IS WRITTEN
THE FUTURE IS WRITTEN
THE FUTURE IS WRITTEN
THE FUTURE
The Future is Sad.
FORTUNE TELLING SERVICES
the future is precious. waste it wisely.
THE FUTURE IS WRITTEN
FORTUNE-TELLING SERVICES W/ WASTEDRITA
FRIDAY: 6 – 7PM
SATURDAY: 6 – 7PM
SUNDAY: NO

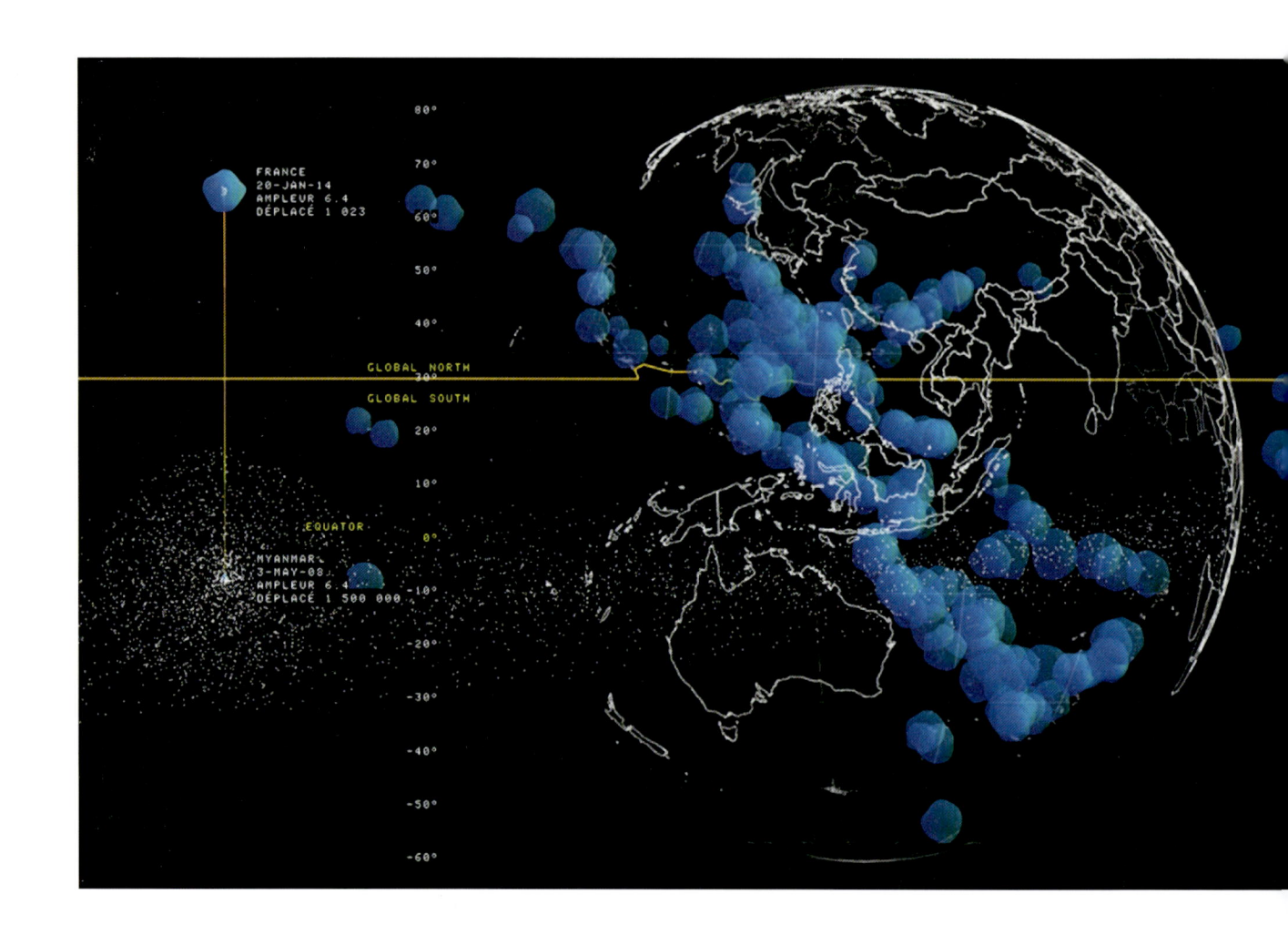

Diller Scofidio + Renfro with Mark Hansen, Laura Kurgan, and Ben Rubin, in collaboration with
Robert Gerard Pietrusko and Stewart Smith, *Exit,* 2014; "Natural Disasters," video still

47

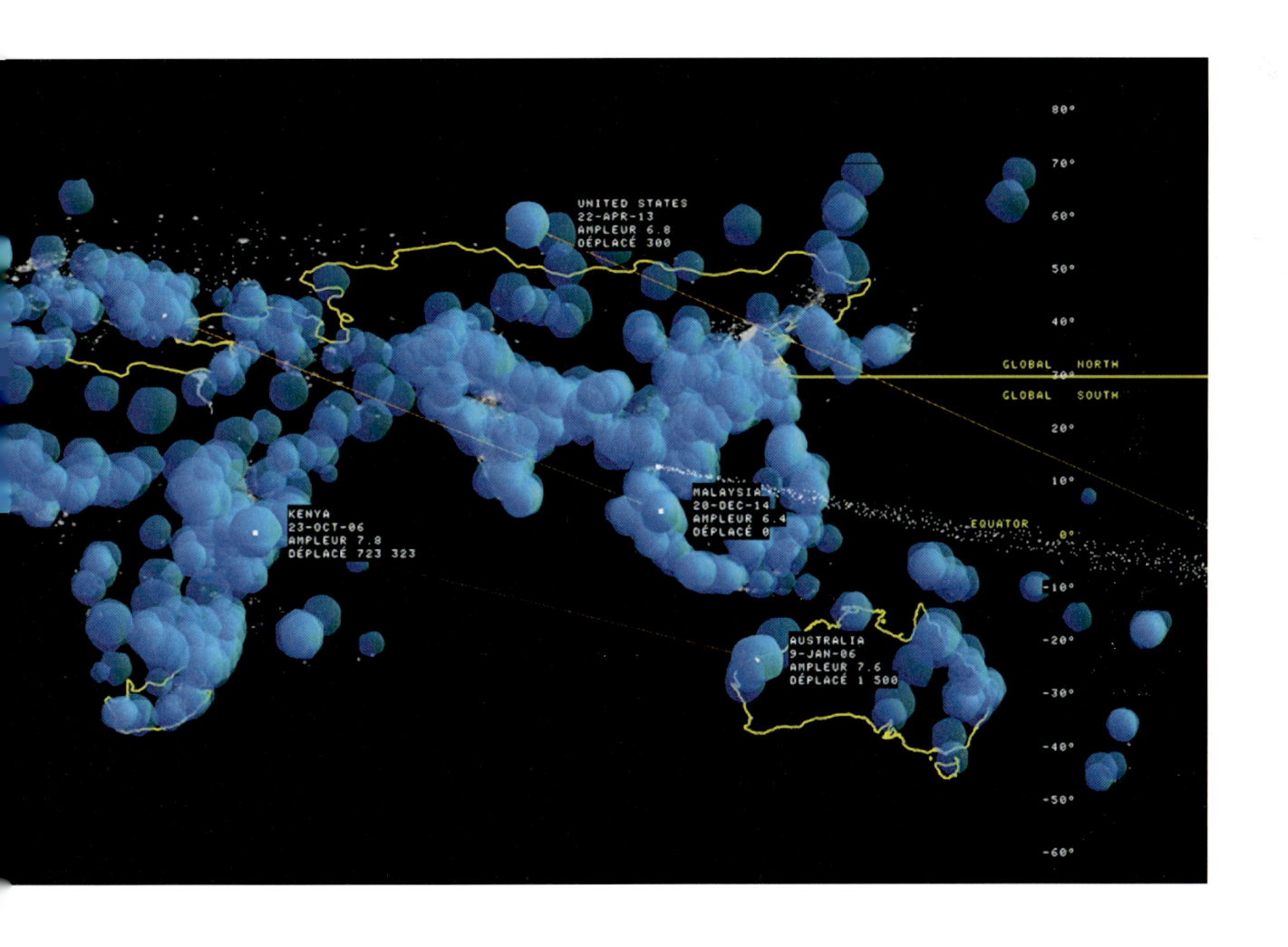

Parsons & Charlesworth, *The BioPhotovoltaics Hacktivist,* from *New Survivalism,* 2014

49

Skrei, *Biogas Power Plant*, 2017

# THE TIMELINESS OF ARCHITECTURE'S ECO-VISIONARY PRACTICES

*AMALE ANDRAOS*

These are complicated times for an eco-visionary. If by "visionary" we mean the potential to imagine future scenarios—actualizing these scenarios virtually in order to render them possible—then the wave of "climate change resistance" that we are experiencing today mind-bogglingly points to the opposite reality. It seems that the more we know about climate change and the more we are able to visibly project its impacts, the less we are able to reach those still "in doubt," leaving us increasingly unable to mobilize with the urgency climate change demands, across scales and territories, nations and organizations.[1] Taking the United States as the most dramatic example of this conundrum, we are faced with both the most advanced climate science research in the world—with its increasingly complex data gathering, sophisticated modeling, and granular projections—and the most aggressive climate change deniers, whose unfettered claims and driven activism have empowered a government with an extreme anti-environmental agenda; a government that continues to giddily deploy devastating policies across the US economy and its territory, and with dramatic consequences well beyond its national boundaries.[2]

Malka Architecture, *The Green Machine*, 2014

Why is this happening? While this has been asked many times since the 2016 US election, the diverse possible causes and answers have yet to be comprehensively examined. If we are to find a way forward then the first and most immediate question to grapple with is who, exactly, this "we," both the subject of and participant in climate change, is. Over and over, the polarization between the country's urban coast and its rural middle has been highlighted as a fundamental and intractable divide on the subject of human-induced climate change, inviting many to declare that climate change is an "elite problem" confined to academics, urban dwellers, and the more seemingly educated populations concentrated in metropolitan coastal areas. An increase in devastating storms has led to a range of names now commonplace in our everyday vocabulary—from Katrina in New Orleans to Sandy in New York, Harvey in Houston, Irma in Miami, and most recently Maria in Puerto Rico—and each of them has rendered the impact of rising waters on coastal cities spectacularly tangible in just a few years. Less eventfully but no less dramatically, we have seen an increase in sustained drought elsewhere, changing agrarian methods and yields as well as affecting social and economic livelihoods deep in the rural inland. And yet, to utter the words "climate change" in these contexts has been at times censored[3] and cast by political demagogy as an "us versus them" ideological issue shrouded by scientific doubt, sophistry, and "fake news" nihilism.[4]

Another issue to consider is that even if a majority of people in the United States today believe human-induced climate change is already impacting lives around the country, most do not believe it will harm them personally.[5] We might be able to attribute this to the country's ethos of exceptionality, which carries from the scale and behavior of its individuals to the historical attitude of the entire nation (and which is one of the plausible explanations for why certain people vote against their own interests).[6] A different reason for this may be related to a problem of risk perception: climate change is devastating in the long term but this devastation is not always visible in the short term. Humans have proven swift to react to perceived imminent threats but slow to mobilize against abstract and gradual dangers—rendering climate change the kind of threat that is most difficult for humans to face.[7] One might even ruminate on the many studies—in literature, philosophy, behavioral studies, economics, and psychoanalysis, to name but a few disciplines of desire and fear—that have long cast doubt on the notion that humans act rationally.[8]

Whatever the reason, the current (extreme) polarization we are witnessing between various forms of knowledge—scientific, abstract, and projective on the one hand, emotional, lived, and of the moment on the other—is an invitation to agree with Naomi Klein, who, at a 2014 conference at Columbia Graduate School of Architecture, Planning, and Preservation, declared that "climate change has a communication problem."[9] While this declaration was met with surprise by the audience at the time, it seems, in retrospect, to be quite true. Scientists' datascapes and infographics trace alarming projections decades into the future, but for too many these forecasts are simply not coming through. This failure of communication, but also of imagination, can be read across multiple channels. First, the all too abstract, distant, and intangible rendering of climate change is failing to register it as a thing that will imminently alter lived experience across place, scale, and time. Second, the affirmation that human behavior is irrational should once and for all undermine the positivist attitude that continues to put forth technocratic approaches as the "solution" to life on earth, from smart cities to exclusively engineered systems. And finally, this latest incarnation of our postmodern society of spectacle as "fake news" is a remarkable twist of irony in today's data and data science-obsessed age of information.

If the age of information is failing to communicate and has discovered its limits, rather than deplore ignorance, arrogance, politics, social and economic inequalities, or human nature—all of which are clearly a part of this failure—it may be useful to consider this strange convergence of events and circumstances as an invitation for new ideas, new kinds of visions, and new cultural imaginations: a timely opportunity to reinvent and hybridize old and new modes of communicating, to open up old and new forms of knowledge, and to engage in old and new forms of practice. This opportunity certainly does not mean casting aside the sciences, data scientists, or engineering solutions—these remain as vital as ever. But it does suggest new possibilities for the humanities, like literature and science fiction, art and architecture practices, and calls especially for a re-examination of architecture's long history of utopian thought—a lineage that includes many failures whose guilty burden we continue to carry, and yet whose power to communicate, mobilize, and expand the possible have largely been abandoned by academic discourse. It is within this framework that it seems worthwhile to revisit what is meant by communication in and through architecture. At a time when everything we imagined we had achieved is crumbling from the resurgence of all that we fantasized was left behind—religion, identity politics, nationalism, fascism, racism, sexism—we are confronted with our own limits and the very real fears that much of what accelerated our connections is now dividing us instead.

It is in this moment, then, contrary to all expectations, that architecture stands to reclaim a territory it once ceded. If architecture embodies the clichéd meeting ground between art and science—recasting problems to offer more than engineered solutions, reframing the sites and scales of interventions, and moving beyond either/or conditions to design ways of holding things together—then now is the time for architecture to bridge the stark oppositions we have constructed for ourselves. If architecture-as-building has never been modern, to borrow Bruno Latour's phrase, then enlisting it today for its capacity to weave together abstraction and material reality, the real and its representation, is critical if we are to bring together various forms of knowing. If architecture-as-practice does all that Dipesh Chakrabarty declares is critical for engaging climate and its impact—thinking across scales of environment; registering local specificities while recognizing the importance of universal aspirations; recognizing our discipline as both particular and synthetic, and able to uniquely design together the multitude of ingredients that the life of species, and geological time, are now (or should be) part of—then now is the time to empower architecture and to cultivate the qualities that it inherently holds and that are currently still only latent.

When considering the expanded field that architecture has become and the expanded practices it has inspired, one can start to trace the potential for architecture to advance new forms of knowledge and action about and around climate change. The return of drawing and a renewed investment in mapping has turned architecture-as-visualization and its uniquely critical engagement with data into one of the most productive forms of architectural research and practice today. Drawing across scales and rendering together the infinite and interconnected relationships of networks of exchange manifest across extensive landscapes and territories, these new forms of visualization offer us layered understandings of planetary politics (resource extractions, forced migrations of humans and animals, labor movements, conflict, and high-speed urbanization) together with the spatial and temporal transformation of our built and unbuilt environments. A renewed engagement with making and material has crystallized the concept of embodied energy, moving buildings out of the static and autonomous frames architects long set around them, and connecting them instead to the infinite geographies and production processes embedded within each one of their parts. Finally, new scalar and systems-thinking design approaches have opened up cross-disciplinary discourses and practices that are not only hybridizing architecture, planning, landscape, and preservation, but also integrating concepts of uncertainty, softness, biology, participation, and temporality to create a new wave of radical experimentation in infrastructure.

While many of these practices might appear to cast architecture as a strictly technological discipline, another strand of practices is simultaneously emerging that is layering narrative on to the work in ways once thought to be either dead or at least frowned upon. Why would architecture continue to be enlisted to communicate, many have asked, when there are so many other ways to do so in our age of information?[10] And yet, over and over again, it is precisely this communicative dimension that architecture has been asked to provide—and it offers an important point of engagement with the complexity that such multi-layered problems demand. Enlisting history to re-imagine forms of architectural communication for the present, especially in regards to eco-visionary work, it is useful to look back at two practices that hybridized modes and mediums, disciplines and practices, building and narrative, architecture and environment, and experience and communication with a clarity, richness, playfulness, and complexity, and that continue to operate as models of eco-visionary engagement today.

The first is the art and architectural practice of Ant Farm, whose pioneering explorations and investments across a wide variety of mediums not only set them apart from their peers at the time, but continue to situate their practice as a singular trajectory—one that announced many future lines of inquiry but never became entrenched in the many new directions it helped launch. Moving seamlessly from drawing to building, from video to performance, and from prolific collage to large-scale mixed-media models, land art, and installations, Ant Farm's short but prolific alternate form of practice blurred the boundaries between art and architecture as well as between architectural practice and political activism in ways reminiscent of emerging contemporary sensibilities.[11]

Charged by the environmental movement that was crystallizing in the late sixties and seventies, Ant Farm developed alongside other visionaries, such as Archigram, Superstudio, and Archizoom, differentiating itself by embracing new forms of media and communication to animate its projects. Whether with the happenings they organized around their 1971 *Inflatables,* the press conference they staged around the launch of *Convention City,* or their obsession with broadcasting evinced in projects such as *Media Burn* and *Media Van,* Ant Farm radically reframed architecture as both object and network, stable and temporary, material and virtual, form and performance, technology and iconicity. Their vision offered certain forms of disciplinary continuity alongside a genuinely counter-cultural stance.[12] This radical

Ant Farm, *Clean Air Pod* at the Air Emergency event, 1970, performance, Lower Sproul Plaza, University of California, Berkeley

WORKac and Ant Farm, *3.C.City: Climate, Convention, Cruise,* 2015

intersection of architecture's technological, semiotic, and formal characteristics and capacities was not coincidental. Rather, Ant Farm saw itself as precisely and uniquely drawing together the divergent legacies of Buckminster Fuller on the one hand and Robert Venturi on the other.[13]

It is this intersection that my own architectural practice was most interested in exploring in our collaboration for the 2015 Chicago Architecture Biennial. With Ant Farm's projects as the subject and Ant Farm members Chip Lord and Curtis Schreier as our design collaborators, we proposed *3.C.City: Climate, Convention, Cruise,* which, as the text of the exhibition suggested, "transforms [censured]'s polemical explorations of a counter-America for a present post-American global context, one in which climate change, rising sea levels and sinking cities are challenging architecture to engage in urgent diplomacy among the species and become an agent for the future."[14] The product of long conversations around the re-drawing of three of Ant Farm's most seminal projects—the *House of the Century,* the *Dolphin Embassy,* and *Convention City*—*3.C.City* nested three scales, house, building, and city, in order to collect the narratives embedded in each of the original projects. Capturing and re-interpreting some of their elements, *3.C.City* registered the "then and now" of environmental engagement together with a shift in the territorial imaginary—from the open landscape of the *Truckstop Network Placemat* (1970) to the planetary scale of climate change and rising waters—to propose new ways of living and interacting across scales, contexts, and species.

Another seminal practice we should revisit with fresh eyes today is Sculpture in the Environment (SITE)—whose work reveals the possibilities of bringing communication and environment together. SITE's most revered early project, the series of big-box showrooms designed for the Best Products Company, registered the postmodern interests of its time to enlist architecture's ability to engage the ordinary as well as embrace its capacity to communicate. But beyond this interest in legibility, SITE's work was unique in tying architecture to environmental art practices outside of it while also openly and polemically mobilizing architecture as critical commentary and as a constant critique of itself.

Triangulating art, architecture, and environment, SITE's practice redefined each field in relation to the other and helped articulate a burgeoning scene of artists and architects who were together offering an alternative to the canonical and mostly formal concerns of art and architecture at the time.[15] Through SITE, James Wines rendered visible approaches to

Buckminster Fuller, *Dome Over Manhattan*, 1960

SITE, *Forest Building,* Best Products Company, Richmond, VA, 1980

formless, conceptual, and critical art and architectural practices—the work, often refreshingly playful and witty, always operated beyond the safe and stable disciplinary boundaries it was recasting. Wines's pioneering concerns with architecture's environmental dimension led to a prolific body of work that mingled architecture and landscape, density and ecology, and infrastructure, public space, and public art well ahead of its time.

Recollecting on some of the practice's radical propositions: as early as 1977, SITE designed and built *Ghost Parking Lot,* still one of the most innovative experiments in public infrastructure, public art, and architecture to this day. In 1981, at the height of postmodern obsessions with historicism, SITE proposed its *Highrise of Homes*—filling Le Corbusier's concrete frame with a stack of suburban homes and lawns. The practice's 1983 proposal for Frankfurt's Museum für Moderne Kunst (Museum of Modern Art) juxtaposed vertical landscape and building well before the integration of "green" architectural materials became *du jour.* And in the early nineties, as formal and digital BLOB mania proliferated, SITE radically reimagined ecology, infrastructure, and architecture with a series of urban interventions, such as the Avenue Five Central Plaza and Water Buildings for the 1992 Seville Universal Expo and Ross's Landing Park and Plaza built that same year. Wines's academic engagement and prolific writing continued SITE's interrogation of "environmental thinking." His early seventies publication entitled ON SITE dedicated its sixth issue to the topic of energy, and his book *Green Architecture* (2000) first defined the idea of ecological architecture and soon became a best seller. The practice's monograph, *Identity and Density* (2006), continues to inspire a new generation.

Architecture is a discipline founded on precedent—and the challenges our discipline faces are unprecedented. Within this seemingly contradictory condition, a genuinely progressive architectural practice locates itself in suspension. Like the two recalled in this essay, it always revisits the past and expands on well-established lineages of thought—keeping its eye on the horizons of our own urgencies and redrawing those horizons as we imagine new architectures that reckon with the increasingly destructive remaking of our planet. It has frequently been observed that "climate" is both real and imagined, in that we can only understand it through models. The role of the eco-visionary today is to model our built environment in a similar spirit: to gather data, to deepen our understanding of ecological networks, to take seriously our projections of what architecture *does* (socially, materially, energetically, environmentally), and all the while refine our means of communication.

The Living, *Hy-Fi*, 2014

1   While the Paris Agreement sets a two-degree limit, recent modeling suggests that we are on track to exceed the worst predictions. See Robinson Meyer, "Avoiding Two Degrees of Warming 'Is Now Totally Unrealistic,'" *The Atlantic,* June 3, 2017, https://www.theatlantic.com/science/archive/2017/06/oppenheimer-interview/529083/ (accessed October, 2017).

2   Since taking office, Trump has continued to overturn and rollback policies set by the Obama administration to combat climate change. For a running list, see Michael Greshko et al., "A Running List of How Trump is Changing the Environment," *National Geographic,* February 13, 2018, https://news.nationalgeographic.com/2017/03/how-trump-is-changing-science-environment/; Nadja Popovich et al., "67 Environmental Rules on the Way Out Under Trump," *The New York Times,* January 31, 2018, https://www.nytimes.com/interactive/2017/10/05/climate/trump-environment-rules-reversed.html?mtrref=www.google.com&_r=0 (accessed October, 2017).

3   In fact, the governor of Florida banned the terms "climate change" and "global warming" in 2015. See Tristram Korten, "In Florida, Officials Ban Term 'Climate Change,'" *Miami Herald,* March 8, 2015, http://www.miamiherald.com/news/state/florida/article12983720.html (accessed October, 2017).

4   See Hiroko Tabuchi, "In America's Heartland, Discussing Climate Change Without Saying 'Climate Change,'" *The New York Times,* January 28, 2017, https://www.nytimes.com/2017/01/28/business/energy-environment/navigating-climate-change-in-americas-heartland.html (accessed October, 2017).

5   New data released by the Yale Program on Climate Change Communication gives the most detailed view yet of public opinion on global warming. See Jennifer Marlon et al., "Geographic Variation in Opinions on Climate Change at State and Local Scales in the USA," *Nature Climate Change* 5 (April 2015), pp. 596–603.

6   See Michael Moore, "5 Reasons Why Trump Will Win," *michaelmoore.com,* July 2016, https://michaelmoore.com/trumpwillwin/ (accessed October, 2017).

7   Nadja Popovich et al., "How Americans Think About Climate Change, in Six Maps," *The New York Times,* March 21, 2017, https://www.nytimes.com/interactive/2017/03/21/climate/how-americans-think-about-climate-change-in-six-maps.html (accessed October, 2017).

8   Here, the list is long. But a useful contemporary anecdote is found in the calorie labels on menus and packaging, which policy-makers thought would encourage healthy eating. However, various studies have shown the opposite: that in fact people, at the expense of their health, started to buy higher calorie food, with the reasoning that they were getting more value for their money.

9   Naomi Klein et al., "Drain: Planning for Climate Change" (presentation, Columbia University Graduate School of Architecture, Planning, and Preservation, New York, NY, September 24, 2014).

10   Amale Andraos et al., "Postmodern Proceedings: Deforming" (presentation, Princeton University School of Architecture, Princeton, NJ, December 5, 2017).

11   To name just two successful models of this form of engagement and practice, see architecture collective Assemble, winner of the 2015 Turner prize, and artist Theaster Gates, founder of the non-profit Rebuild Foundation. Gates is currently a professor in the Department of Visual Art and director of Arts and Public Life at the University of Chicago.

12   Ant Farm's best-known built work includes *Inflatables* (1971), the *House of the Century* (1972), *Cadillac Ranch Show* (1974), and *Media Burn* (1975). In our conversations, Chip Lord suggested *Convention City* (1972) had initially been a developer's subject of interest and the realization of *Dolphin Embassy* (1974) occupied much of Doug Michel's focus from 1977–78. For more on this see Doug Michel, interview by Constance Lewallen, in *Ant Farm: 1968–1978,* eds. Constance Lewallen and Steve Seid, exh. cat. Berkeley Art Museum (Berkeley, 2004).

13   See for example Felicity D. Scott, *Architecture or Techno-Utopia: Politics after Modernism* (Cambridge, 2010), pp. 180–81. This Buckminster–Venturi intersection was also discussed at length in our conversations in the forthcoming catalogue of the 2015 Chicago Architecture Biennial.

14   WORKac and Ant Farm, *The State of the Art of Architecture* (2015).

15   Through figures and friends such as Emilio Ambasz, Vito Acconci, Ant Farm, Nancy Holt, Mary Miss, Gaetano Pesce, Gordon Matta-Clark, Gianni Pettena, and Robert Smithson, among others.

Superuse, *Harvestmap Platform: Blue City,* 2012–ongoing

Design Crew for Architecture, *Freshwater Factory Skyscraper*, 2010

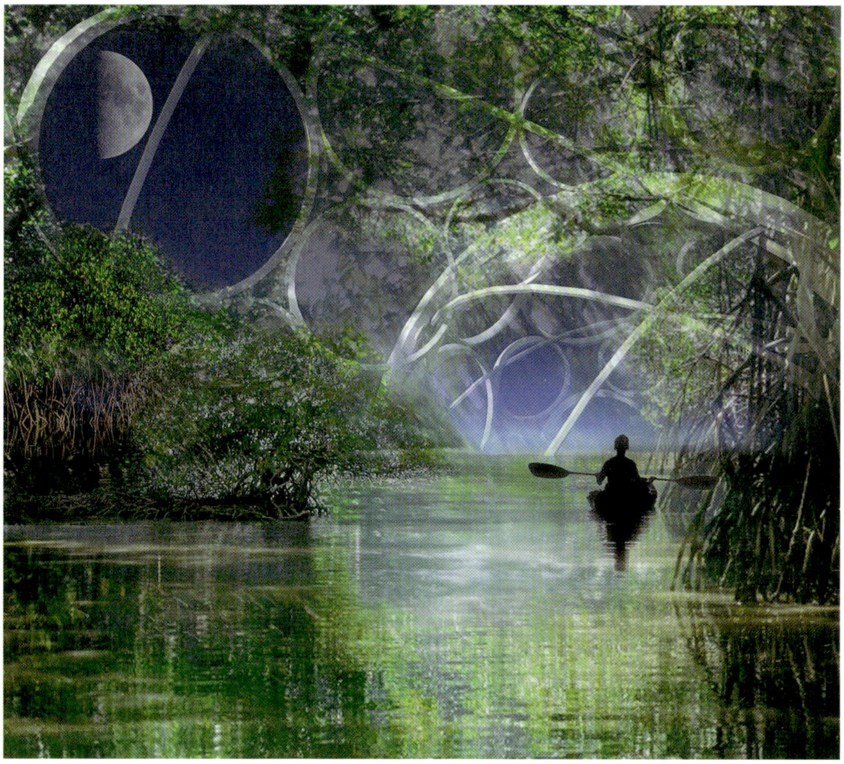

*Stratus Cloud plan*

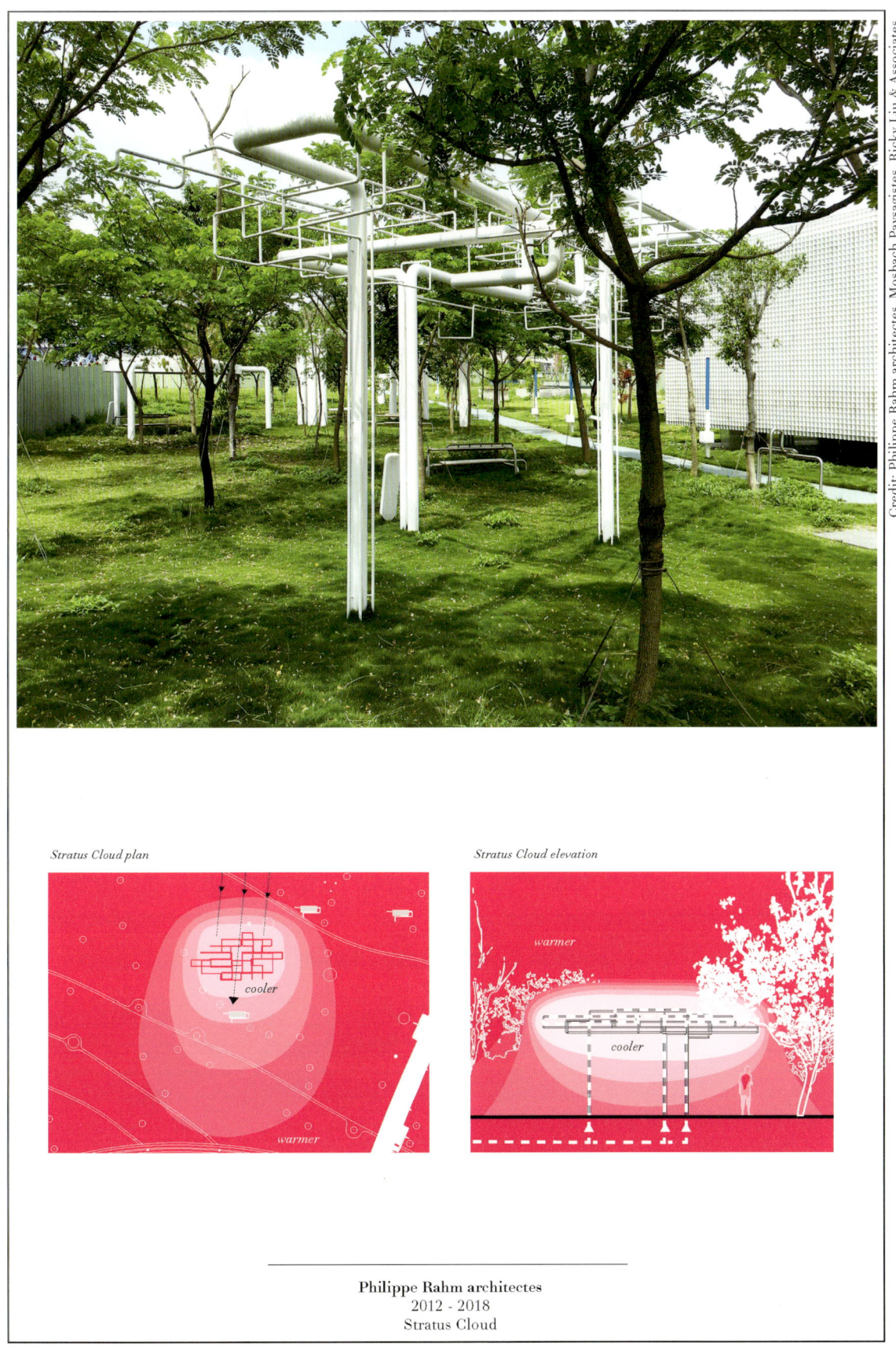

*Stratus Cloud elevation*

Philippe Rahm architectes
2012 - 2018
Stratus Cloud

Philippe Rahm, *Meteorological Architecture*, 2009–11

BIG, *Amager Resource Center*, 2013

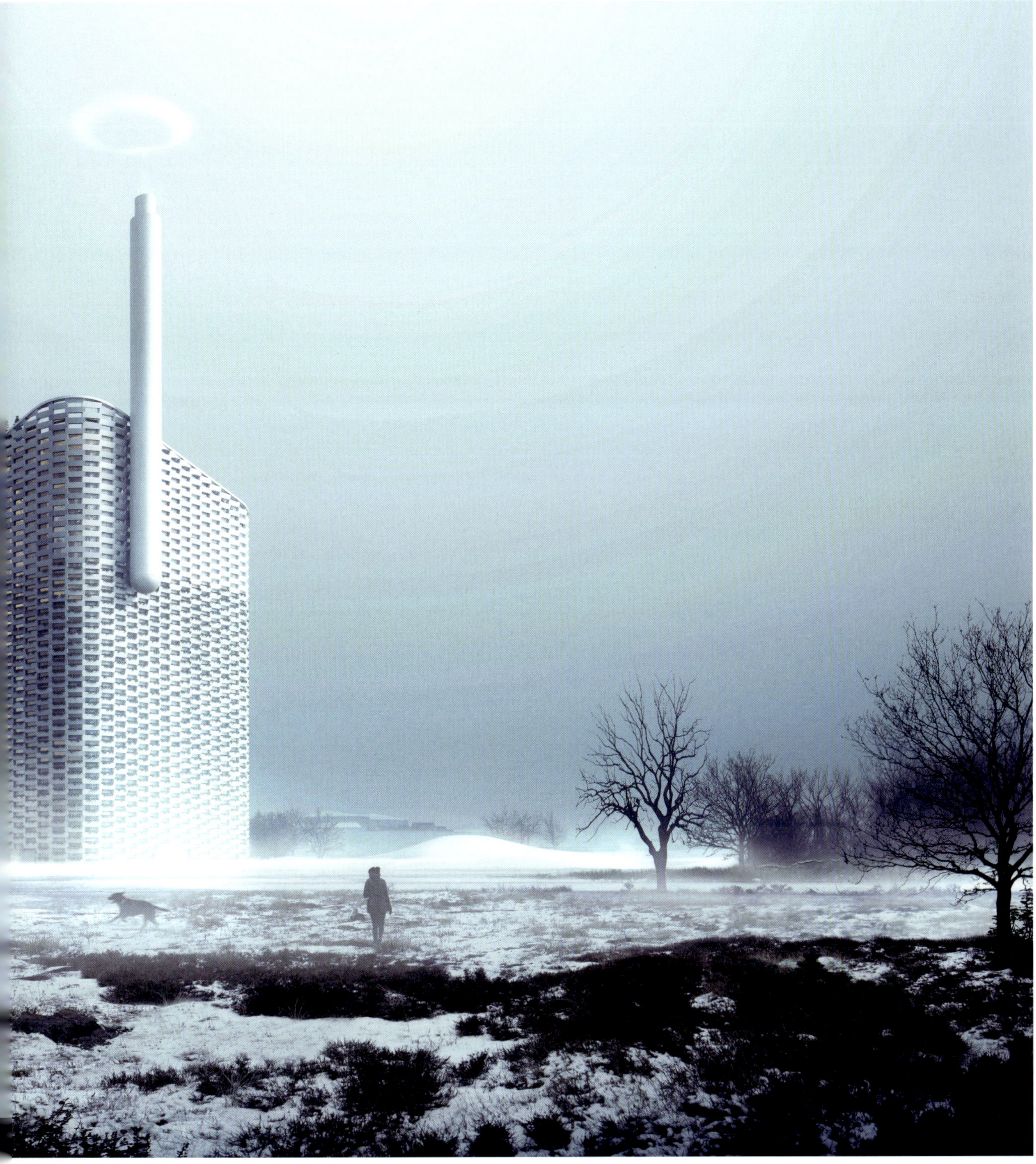

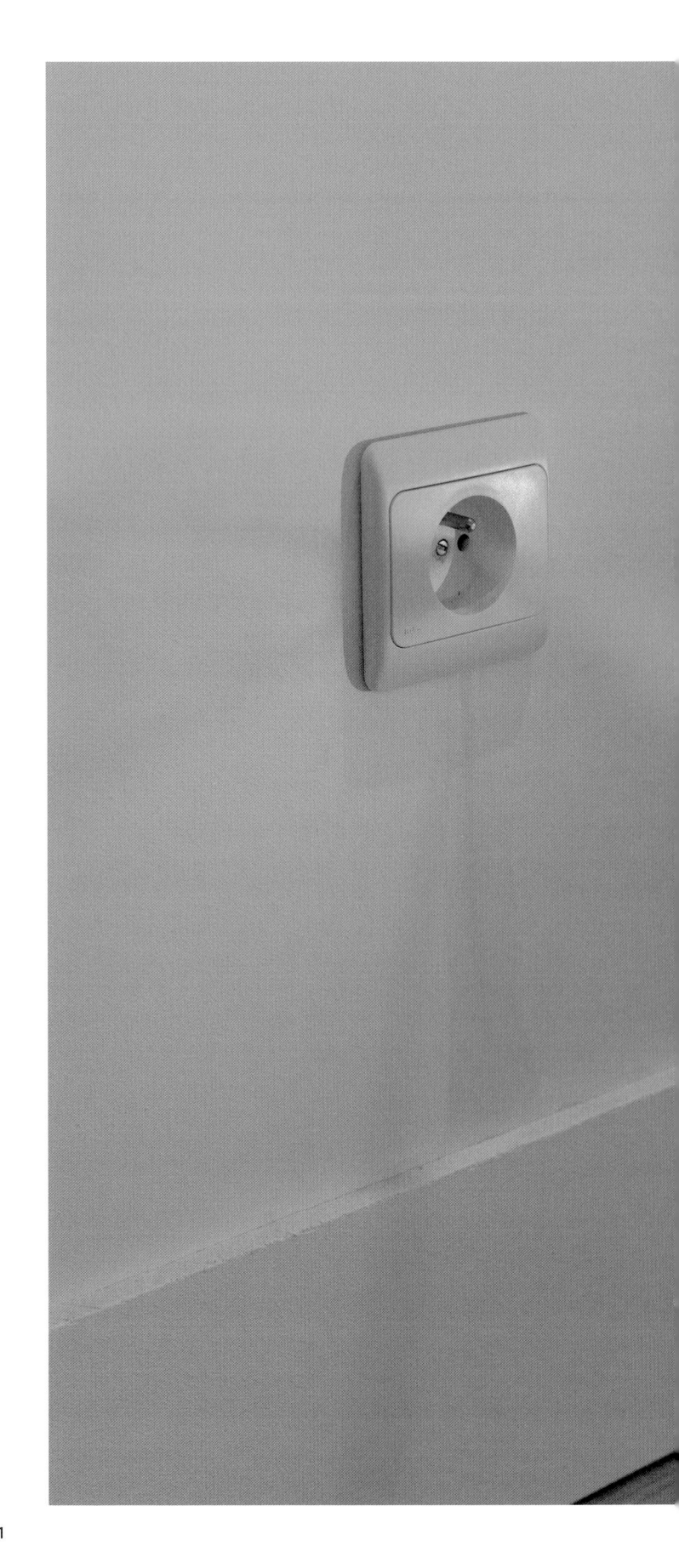

HeHe, *Catastrophes Domestiques N°2: Prise en Charge*, 2011

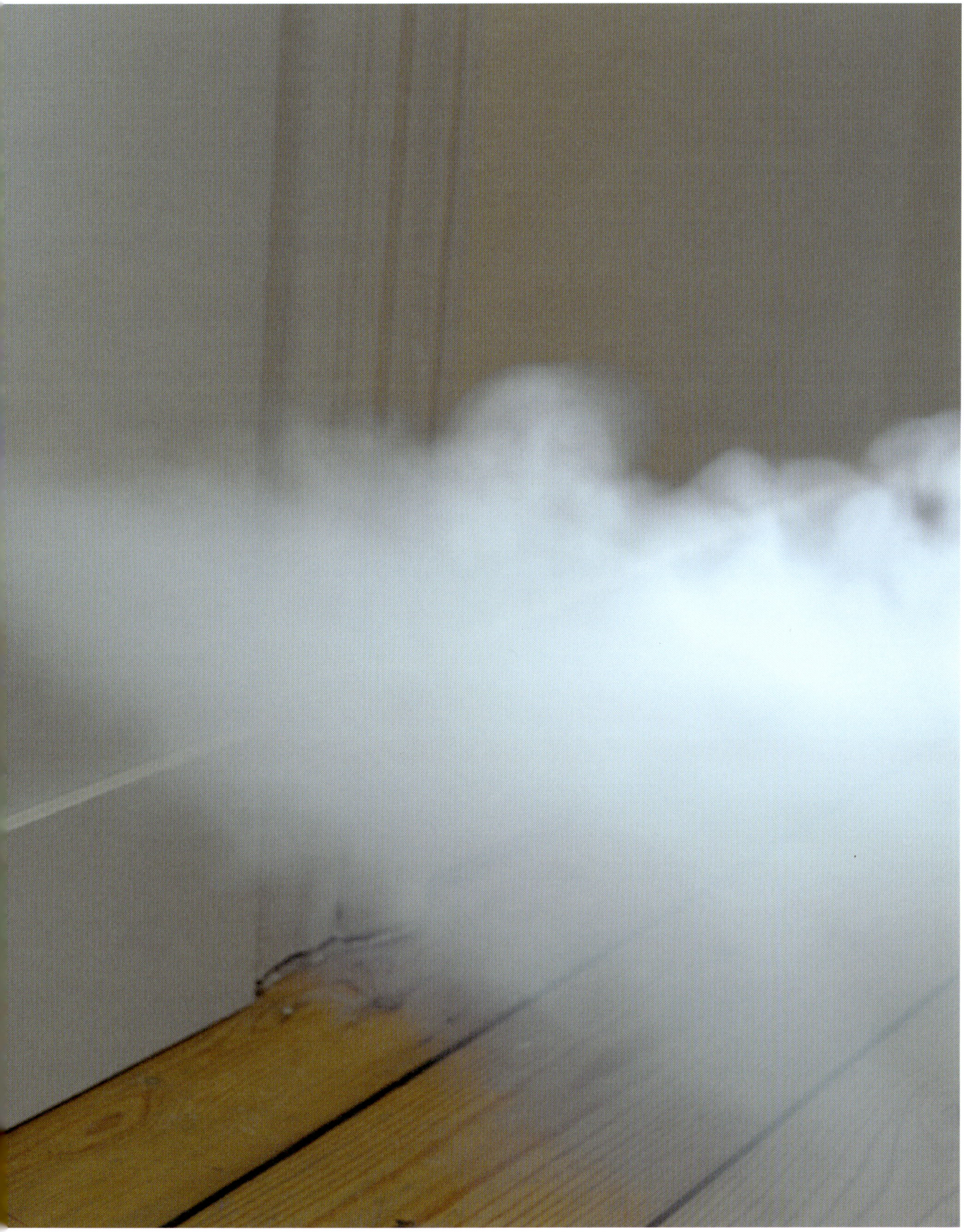

# ECO-VISIONARIES: ART AND ARCHITECTURE AFTER THE ANTHROPOCENE

*MARIANA PESTANA*

In February 2000, in Cuernavaca, Mexico, the atmospheric chemist and Nobel Prize-winner Paul Crutzen declared that we were living in a new geological epoch, which he called the Anthropocene. This was at a conference of the International Geosphere-Biosphere Programme, and the new term was printed two years later in an article in *Nature* journal.[1] In containing the prefix *anthropos,* meaning "human being," the term defines a geological epoch marked by human action, confirming that the activities of humankind have had a deep effect on the environment. Crutzen assigned the start of the Anthropocene to the year 1784 when James Watt patented the steam engine, symbolic of the start of industrialization. Described as "a real product of the enlightenment,"[2] Watt could not have imagined that his invention would one day be the symbol of technological progress, and thus assigned the responsibility of opening up a new geological era. Leaving aside the controversies about the specifics of the term and the date to which its beginning should be attributed, it is clear that we have established a link between technological progress and climate change.

John Gerrard, *Western Flag (Spindletop, Texas)*, 2017, video stills

Ornaghi & Prestinari, *Asmatico*, 2015–16

Inventions of the eighteenth century, like the steam engine, were produced alongside philosophies of enlightenment that promoted values of rationality and ideas of technological advancement and progress. What systems of thought might the ecological awareness of the twenty-first century inspire? Now, after the Anthropocene, we are faced with a paradox: if the ideals of reason and science that stimulate technological progress can be directly linked to environmental destruction, where do we head? What are the alternative orienting principles of reason, objectivity, and rationality? This exhibition, taking place at MAAT in Lisbon, seeks to address this paradox through the ecological visions of art and architecture. In the subjective, the fluctuating, the unstable images of ecology captured by works of art and architecture, we seek to rescue a sense of hope in the future. Divided into four sections—disaster, confluence, extinction, adaptation—the exhibition rescues a critical optimism from the shadows of enlightenment.

**DISASTER**

Ecosystems as far as the Amazon rainforest and the Artic are changing dramatically. Mountain glaciers are retreating and water supply is shortening. Weather is shifting, presenting threats to food production. Sea levels are rising, increasing the risk of flooding. From 1880 to 2012, the average global temperature increased by 0.85°C. Growing CO2 emissions, which contribute to raising the average global temperature on Earth, are the product of burning fossil fuels.[3] A direct link can be established between technological progress and global warming. The repercussions will transcend generations. Nature is no longer something that we can watch safely from a distance, it is slowly entering through the window to haunt our dreams of progress and comfort.

In 1901, an enormous geyser of oil exploded from a drilling site at Spindletop Hill, a mound created by an underground salt deposit located near Beaumont, southeastern Texas, United States. Reaching a height of more than 40 meters and producing close to 100,000 barrels a day, the geyser was more powerful than any previously seen in the world. A booming oil industry soon grew up around the oil field at Spindletop, and many of the major oil companies in America, including Gulf Oil, Texaco, and Exxon, can trace their origins there. In one day, the Lucas Geyser, as it was called, produced more oil than the rest of the world's oilfields combined at the time.[4] Nowadays, the oil deposits are exhausted. It is this deserted landscape of Spindletop that makes the background to John Gerrard's work *Western Flag* (p. 73). The video installation depicts a virtual simulation of the Texan landscape and on it a pole bearing a flag of perpetually renewing, pressurized black smoke. Against a depopulated backdrop, the flag evokes a sublime image. The thick black smoke blows in a mesmerizing, hypnotic continuous loop, as if the source is never exhausted. In doing so, it mirrors the Western unconscious. Because despite knowing that fossil fuel is finite, the so-called "developed" world continues to exploit it as if there was no end. Gerrard's work uncomfortably aestheticizes oil as a structure of power that fuelled the expansion of human enterprise.

The image of smoke as a manifestation of unconscious consumption is further imbued in HeHe's work *Catastrophes Domestiques,* (pp. 70–71) albeit, as the title suggests, at the domestic scale of the home. The Paris-based artist duo did a series of experiments that draw attention to the energetic consumption of everyday appliances. *Prise en Charge* is a power plug that exhales smoke, thus giving consumers back the pollution created by their energetic intake. This humorous yet disturbing piece makes a straightforward link between the luxury of technology and its consequence. Often invisible to the consumer, the consequence—here represented in the form of polluting smoke—comes back to haunt the comfort of the home. It is also as a haunting element that smoke populates Ornaghi & Prestinari's conceptual architectural models: *Paesaggio* (p. 74) depicts an imaginary landscape with smoking chimneys. The puffing and wheezing smoke, often excluded from architectural representations, is portrayed as an intrinsic element of the romantic landscape. As such, the familiar image of the smoke disturbs the architectural model, rendering it strange. Design Earth, the practice of architects Rania Ghosn and El Hadi Jazairy, renders visible the waste infrastructures of urban landscapes. Their installation *Trash Peaks* subverts the object of the *irworobongdo,* a traditional Korean folding screen that portrays a political cosmology composed of the sun, moon, and a landscape of five peaks. They introduce a series of six highly stylized landforms to this traditional composition, placing the undesired matter of waste management—its flows, ecologies, logistics, managerial structures, and labor—at center stage.

Revealing the smoke, machines, instruments, and architectures that make our twenty-first-century comfort possible, these projects bring forward a kind of ecological unconscious. Each focusing on a different scale and aspect of technological development, together they draw a picture of what it takes, what lies beneath, and what is at stake when we go about our every day.

**CONFLUENCE**

The effects of climate change are felt in places far from those in which the cause is produced. Ecological formations have a global dimension. Complex networks of geopolitical events interlink Northern and Southern hemispheres. Ecology takes up mystical and political forms, as Édouard Glissant put it.[5] In its mystical form, ecology privileges notions of the Earth as a sacred territory belonging to its "native" inhabitants, who originally settled the land and thus possess a sacred right to the territory. In its political form, it captures the stories of people deprived of their own land by way of processes such as colonialization (I would add, more recently climate migration and ecocide), and thus destabilizes the first. Against a model of rootedness, Glissant emphasizes the need for a rhizomatic ecology grounded on relations of solidarity between all the lands, across the whole Earth. In such relational geographies, the confluence of sites of cause and effect (of climate change) is not always rendered visible.

Consider, for example, Territorial Agency's work *Museum of Oil* (p. 78), which depicts satellite aerial images of large oil reserves next to on-the-ground reports from people affected by the exploitation of the reserves. Workers, migrants: those who labor for the extraction of oil or who are displaced by the consequences of the extraction. Indeed, the sites where the fuel of progress burns and those where the fuel of progress is extracted often do not coincide. Profits tend to be made in the sites of fuel burning, at the expense of the labor and resources of the sites of fuel extraction. Think of the empire of South African Elon Musk, the hero of sustainability. His dream of Tesla is a dream of electric cars, itself supported by the

Design Earth, *Trash Peaks*, 2017

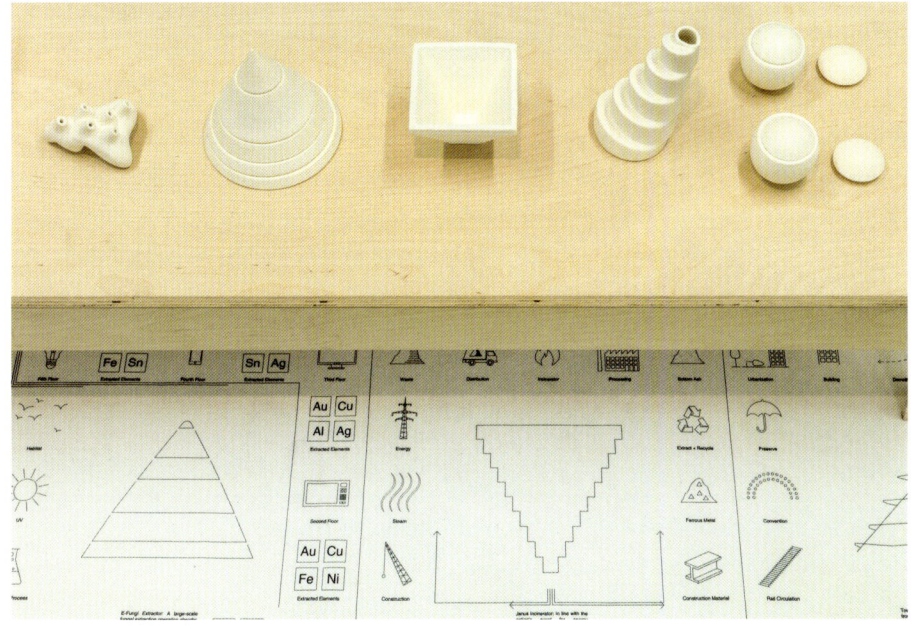

Territorial Agency, *Museum of Oil*, 2016

idea of a Gigafactory of electric batteries. But these batteries are made of lithium, which is extracted in Chile and Bolivia. Unknown Fields Division (p. 81), a research unit at the Architectural Association in London led by Kate Davies and Liam Young, has documented this process. In the summer of 2015 they traveled with their students through the lithium mines of Bolivia and the Atacama Desert to explore the infrastructure lying beneath our dreams of clean energy. Buried beneath Salar de Uyuni, the world's largest salt flat, they observed over half of the world's reserves of lithium. This substance is the key ingredient of batteries, which in turn powers our mobile phones, laptops, and electric cars. The documentation of their *Lithium Dreams Expedition* reveals the extraction process of evaporation: a patchwork ocean of ponds, some drained and the task transferred to the next in line each month, their color changing as the lithium concentration rises. Mine workers monitor this fifteen-month process that develops across the ponds. The artwork poignantly shows that even the cleanest energy utopias have dramatic consequences of material, resource, and economic exploitation. It draws a relational geography that connects the consumption of batteries in the Northern Hemisphere to the extraction of resources in the south. Because, as Portuguese sociologist Boaventura Sousa Santos states, the abyssal lines that were once drawn to divide geographies of north and south are still at play today,[6] and they are visible in many of the projects highlighted in this section. Take, for example, Kiluanji Kia Henda's *Havemos de Voltar (We Shall Return)* (pp. 88–89), a video work that, in a political metaphor, draws a poignant difference between Portuguese, Angolan, and Chinese conceptions of nature and development. Set in a natural history museum and narrated by a *palanca-negra,* this work presents the triad of conflicting desires at play in contemporary Luanda. In fact, some of the most compelling environmental work by artists and architects maps out links between coexisting political ecologies. Diller Scofidio + Renfro's major project *Exit* (pp. 46–47) quantifies and displays contemporary mass global movements of migration across continents, as prompted by political and environmental crises, in a living archive of news footage, statistics, photographs, and documentaries. Carolina Caycedo's cartographies (pp. 98–99) perhaps more directly show how, at the local scale of communities, resistance to the pressures of technological progress is enacted. Having researched the impact of dam construction in Colombia and Brazil, she documents personal stories of opposition to engineering projects, which are often fought with everyday actions, such as permanence at home to avoid eviction and the documentation of struggles in the form of local crafts.

These projects engage with the climate as something dependent on the relations of geographies and people. They offer interdependent models that reactivate an aesthetic of the land, or Earth, or nature, shifting away from the notion of territory as a place defined by its limits and conceiving instead of the Earth as a boundless space of turbulence.

**EXTINCTION**

It is estimated that at the current rate, twenty percent of the planet's species will have disappeared by 2030.[7] In the last few decades, the extinction rate of species has been from 100 to 1,000 times greater than the geological norm, leading biologists to consider the possibility of the "sixth extinction" since the appearance of life on Earth. The last extinction, which wiped out dinosaurs, among others, happened sixty-five million years ago. This means that in the coming decades societies will have to face changes to the state of the planet—such as a rise in the average temperature—of which the human species, as young as only two and a half million years old, has never experienced, and for which it is not culturally or biologically adapted.[8] This calls for a new understanding of humanity and of the human condition.

At once alarming and witty, Rimini Protokoll's theater installation *win > < win* (p. 150) delivers a dramatic experience where species compete for their ecosystem. It departs from the success of jellyfish, a species that have been around for 670 million years, against all the threats of global warming, such as the rise in water temperature and decrease in oxygen levels. Developed in collaboration with marine biologists and animal keepers, this disturbing work presents jellyfish as the only likely survivor of a mass extinction, and humans as a fragile species on the verge of disappearance.[9] Then there is Eva Papamargariti's *Precarious Inhabitants* (p. 154), which addresses issues of symbiosis and transformation between humans and other artificial and biological entities, proposing yet another view on the human condition. With her background in architecture, Papamargariti's artworks attribute agency to a variety of entities—material, live, organic, digital, and artificial. "Some lands never forget what you do to them," says a disembodied voice in the video work. In this bizarre fluidity of mutating actual and fictional settings, objects of the living world are interrelated and ambivalent, warning us of the future toxic progenies of a distressed, human-shaped environment. Even less hopeful is a twenty-minute film by Jeremy Shaw, *Liminals* (p. 82). "Our extinction is a quantifiable certainty," says the narrator of an imaginary future where a cult develops among society to activate a lost sense of religious belief. Set in a world where the singularity[10] is no longer just a Silicon Valley idea but an established order, the science-fiction documentary portrays a group of people called "liminals" that dance and perform rituals in an attempt to access a realm of consciousness with the potential to save humanity. Their language is reminiscent of the Black Lodge sequences in David Lynch's *Twin Peaks* (where actors speak backwards with a machinic overtone). It puts forward an image of the future in which machines seem to have dominated the world, with their language adopted by humans who live in a hedonistic state of awaiting the end, their only hope being some kind of supernatural redemption. Expecting a transcendental miracle, they push for the world beyond.

Each of these projects provokes us to imagine a world where humans are less important, and less detached from their environment. They invite us to revise our conceptions of what humanity means.

**ADAPTATION**

We used to think of humanity as something defined in opposition to nature. Reason and soul divided us from the rest of the world. But the Anthropocene has made us aware of the extent to which the Earth and humans are interdependent. To survive, we must become earthbound. In other words, our species will have to adapt to the environment that it transformed. We are in it, and we must find a way to inhabit this Earth of today. Giuseppe Tomasi di Lampedusa's dictum that "everything must change so that everything can stay the same" has become a historical maxim quoted again and again to describe the resourceful ways of power in politics. But it is perhaps also helpful in the discussion of the current state of affairs of our species.

Unknown Fields Division, *The Breast Milk of the Volcano,* 2016–18, video stills

Jeremy Shaw, *Liminals,* 2017, video stills

If we have designed our own extinction, can we design our way out of it? There are those who believe that it is possible to reverse the course of the future by protecting existing biodiversity from further human impact and sustaining what already lives. And there are those who believe in the use of genetic engineering as a means to design new biodiversity to ensure that humans can live longer on the planet. Alexandra Daisy Ginsberg is a designer, artist, and writer who has developed an experimental practice to imagine possible futures. Her work *Designing for the Sixth Extinction* (pp. 86–87) discusses the aesthetics and ethics of nature in a synthetic biological future: what would novel species look like? Would they be "alive"? Would an industrialized nature really benefit society? She draws and creates images of these potential new species, modeled on fungus, bacteria, invertebrates, and mammals, that she calls "ecological machines," and which fill the void left by extinct species, or offer protection against harmful invasive species, diseases, and pollution. By making these engineering fictions palpable in visual depictions, Ginsberg invites spectators to think critically about the futures being presented to them by scientists and to speculate about their potential consequences.

The United Nations predicted that, at this rate, there will not be enough food to feed the planet in 2050.[11] So perhaps the first mode of adaptation should be to radically change our diet and/or digestive system. Such is the provocation set up by Dunne & Raby's work *Foragers,* part of their *Designs for an Overpopulated Planet* series (p. 85). This speculative work is composed of a series of objects designed for a future where humans extract nutritional value from synthetic biology and develop new digestive systems like those of other mammals, birds, fish, and insects. Equipped with DIY devices, the future foragers imagined by Dunne & Raby create microbial stomach bacteria, as well as electronic and mechanical devices that maximize the nutritional value of the urban environment where they live. Whereas *Foragers* suggests that our adaptation will involve biological changes and body extensions that allow us to find nutrients inaccessible to us today, projects such as Philippe Rahm's *Meteorological Architecture* (p. 67) suggests that we might engineer weather and geology to suit our needs. To design the environment around us may have proven to be the wrong path, but some believe that if we have entered this spiral of designing the world, we now must take it to the end. But perhaps it is time to abandon the Western hubristic dreams of domination of the planet. One of Zak Ové's *Lost Souls* (p. 149) sculptures portrays a young black boy dressed in *Mad Max*-styled armor made of noise cancelling headphones, a toy airplane, cars, a pilot's oxygen mask, and other paraphernalia. The precarious costume evokes the Trinidadian Carnival and the artist's origins, but also the contemporary excesses of consumerism, remnants of the fragile blend of politics and history that informs contemporary globalization. In the other Trinidad, in Colorado, there is a river called Purgatoire, originally named "Rio de las Ánimas Perdidas en Purgatorio" (River of the Lost Souls in Purgatory). As the story goes, the name of the river refers to a group of Spanish gold-seekers who mysteriously disappeared along the canyon. Some say that, attempting to travel down the stream in boats, they were wrecked among the rapids. Others argue that they lost their provisions and starved in the desert, or that they were attacked by Indigenous Americans. No one knows what happened. Do Ové's *Lost Souls* evoke the greed of Western exploration? Do they announce a post-apocalyptic state of global scarcity?

One thing is certain: in the future that awaits us we will be a precarious species fighting for our own subsistence, and our only hope is to make friends with the Earth below our feet.

The processes of ecological becoming are dependent on the way that we—as citizens, as crowds, as a species—decide to make sense of our own humanity. Is humankind, as the philosopher Timothy Morton proposes, a form of solidarity with others, and other species? Is ecology, as Glissant proposed, a form of interrelated lands that do not belong to any one species? What kind of futures would such a combined model of solidarity and collective ownership point towards? Such possibilities are already inscribed in the present constitution of the world, emerging in the imaginary landscapes of artworks and the fictional ecologies of architectural propositions. What does it take for the fictional to be enacted? What kind of energy is needed for the possible to be actualized? Perhaps it relies on a political potency less sanitized by the numbers and data of scientists and engineers, and instead distilled by the tortuous, grimy, and ambivalent encounters between ecologies of between. Between art and architecture, digital and physical, biological and synthetic, north and west, feet and Earth.

---

1  Christophe Bonneuil and Jean Baptiste Fressoz, *The Shock of the Anthropocene* (London, 2016), pp. 3–4.

2  Robin McKie, "James Watt and the Sabbath Stroll that Created the Industrial Revolution," *The Observer,* May 29, 2015, https://www.theguardian.com/technology/2015/may/29/james-watt-sabbath-day-fossil-fuel-revolution-condenser (accessed November 27, 2017).

3  "Climate Change," United Nations (website), http://www.un.org/en/sections/issues-depth/climate-change/ (accessed October 10, 2017).

4  "Spindletop," History Channel (website), http://www.history.com/topics/spindletop (accessed November 20, 2017).

5  Édouard Glissant, *Poética da Relação* (Porto, 2011), pp. 141–42.

6  Boaventura Sousa Santos, "Para além do pensamento abissal: das linhas globais a uma ecologia de saberes," *Novos Estudos CEBRAP* 79 (2007).

7  Bonneuil and Fressoz 2016 (see note 1), p. 7.

8  Ibid., p. 24.

9  *win > < win* is an installation piece commissioned for the exhibition *After the End of the World,* curated by José Luis de Vicente and produced by the Centre de Cultura Contemporània de Barcelona with FACT+BLUECOAT+RIBA NORTH in Liverpool. It will be on display at MAAT for the duration of the *Eco-Visionaries* exhibition.

10  The technological singularity is the idea that technological progress in artificial intelligence will reach a tipping point where a super intelligence will develop among machines, thus rendering them exponentially "smarter" than humans.

11  "How to feed the world in 2050," Food and Agriculture Organization of the United Nations, http://www.fao.org/fileadmin/templates/wsfs/docs/expert_paper/How_to_Feed_the_World_in_2050.pdf (accessed November 20, 2017).

Dunne & Raby, *Designs for an Overpopulated Planet: Foragers*, 2009

Alexandra Daisy Ginsberg, *Designing for the Sixth Extinction*, 2013–15

87

Kiluanji Kia Henda, *Havemos de Voltar (We Shall Return)*, 2017, video stills

UM SÓ POVO   UMA SÓ NAÇÃO

Ana Vaz and Tristan Bera, *A Film, Reclaimed,* 2015, video stills

Should we still speak of globality?

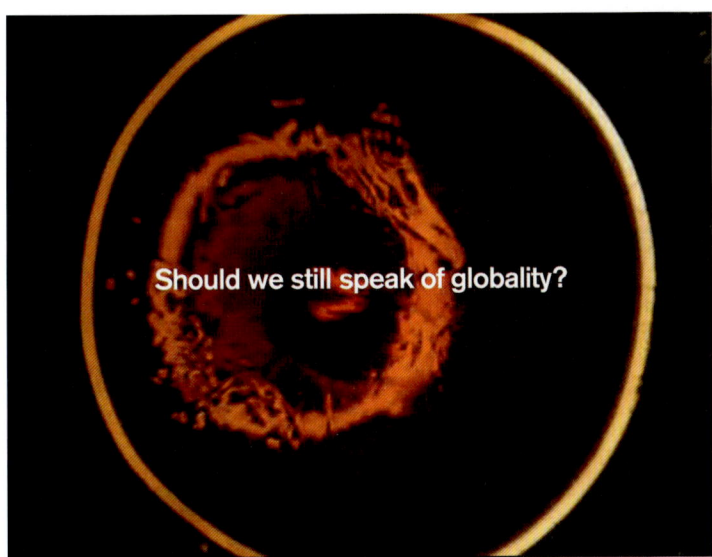

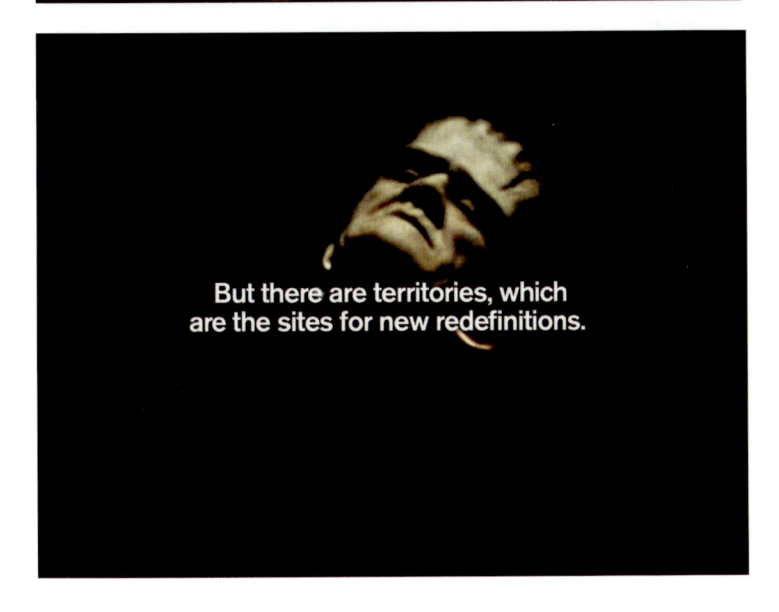

But there are territories, which are the sites for new redefinitions.

# OUR PLACE ON EARTH

SOFIA JOHANSSON

We can all probably recognize the feeling that the world's collected ecological problems tower above us like a dark, threatening cloud whose dimensions are impossible to fathom. The feeling that no matter what I do it is only a drop in the ocean, it does not make any real difference. This may give us a guilty conscience because we know that we are responsible for most of the problems but lack the ability to solve them. It is a feeling of impotence, which easily leads to passiveness.

It requires an effort to not just give up, feeling dejected and helpless. In Bildmuseet's version of *Eco-Visionaries,* the epithet "visionary" is applied to people who, in spite of this seemingly hopeless situation, still manage to do something, think creatively, spawn new ideas to counteract apathy, and suggest new solutions or alternative ways of relating to the world.

Many thinkers have analyzed the situation with the objective of proposing methods to better understand and identify new ways of facing that which appears to be overwhelming. The aim is to make us not feel at a loss when faced with a seemingly inevitable disaster. Many of these thinkers agree that we should stop being so anthropocentric. We should stop seeing ourselves as a separate entity whose interests override everything else. Stop separating nature and culture and instead think about what is best for this world that we share. Several of them criticize the capitalist system, which rarely supports alternatives that promote well-functioning ecosystems.

Leena and Oula-Antti Valkeapää, *Manifestations*, 2017, video still

In *The Three Ecologies*,[1] Félix Guattari explains that the ecological crisis is the result of "Integrated World Capitalism," and proposes that the world needs an ecological philosophy, an "ecosophy," for us to understand and accept that we human beings are only one species of all the living creatures on the earth and should act accordingly. Inspired by Gregory Bateson,[2] he employs the concept of ecology in a wider sense—in addition to nature ecology he also uses concepts such as social ecology and mental ecology—to describe the systems that form relationships and human subjectivity. That is, ecologies in diametrically distinct scales that are inevitably interconnected and affect one another. The artists we have invited to this exhibition work on several of these levels simultaneously, suggesting, in words and actions, steps towards a more sustainable approach to ecologies and our place on earth.

With their poetic video work *Manifestations,* the artist Leena Valkeapää and her reindeer-herding husband, Oula-Antti Valkeapää (p. 93), propose a way of approaching ecological thinking through a close study of the surrounding nature and by acknowledging that they are part of it. The work combines images and text messages sent by Oula-Antti Valkeapää to Leena Valkeapää during his working days in the mountains and forests of the northernmost part of Finland. The brief texts comprise intimate observations of the wonders of nature, existential ruminations, and humorous reflections. Depicted in images and words, the work displays humility towards the vast expanses, the animals, and nature.

Elin Már Øyen Vister's sound piece *Sirkelens ontologi forteller* (The Ontology of the Circle Recounts) also reminds us that other mental ecologies are possible. The sound work is designed as a polyphonic composition, which, in the form of a chant, tells us about the perspective of sustainability in the ontology of the circle, and which invokes goddesses from Sami and Norse mythology. The work was created with inspiration from a reconciliation process between the Sami people and the Norwegian government. This invocation of Sami and Norse mythology constitutes a comment on the colonization of Sami territories and their forced conversion to Christianity, emphasizing how a different ontology came to the fore, which here stands for negative aspects such as hierarchies and conflict, in contrast to the traditional Sami ontology in which rounded lines—such as spheres, eggs, and waves—are regarded as the natural forms that, according to the arrangement of the choir, "foster coherence and not conflict" when they meet. In the work, the Sami and Norse goddesses make a common cause in order to save Mother Earth.

With the objective of presenting their knowledge to an international conference, the

Elin Már Øyen Vister at work

French ecologist Samuel Roturier interviewed three reindeer herders from the Sirges Sami Village in Norrbotten, Sweden, for his film *Working with Nature—Sami Reindeer Herders and Biodiversity in the Boreal Forest.*[4] In the film, the reindeer herders share their special knowledge of why biological diversity in the forest is important for reindeer herding, explaining, among other things, how different forest types affect snow conditions and thus grazing possibilities. They also challenge short-term capitalist thinking and the accepted view on profitability, and propose alternative prioritizations that could lead to a more sustainable future. Reindeer herder Jakob Nygård analyses and summarizes the short-sighted planning for mine exploitation in the middle of reindeer pastureland and proposes a vision for a long-term sustainable future:

Sami reindeer-herder Lars-Evert Nutti reflects on the scarcity of arboreal lichen in today's pine forests. Arboreal lichen is an important feeding resource for reindeer in winter, especially when ground lichen becomes inaccessible to them due to hard or deep snow cover

> "The argument you hear in relation to mining versus reindeer herding is…. They say, for example, that in Gallók there will be 300 jobs for 15 years. Sure, I say. But reindeer herding means 15 jobs for 300 years. That's an equal amount of jobs and we get to keep the nature."[5]

It is simple mathematics and should not be a sensational statement, but daring to say it and daring to believe that a different value system is possible still seems radical.

In the research for *Eco-Visionaries,* the concept of "ecosystem services" emerged as a conspicuous symptom of capitalist structures. Ecosystem services is a term for the "services" that nature performs, such as pollination, water purification, photosynthesis, and so on—functions that are essential for the wellbeing of ecosystems. The concept was invented to make it possible to put a price on our benefits of nature's functions. For example, if there are no longer any pollinators for fruit trees, a human being has to do the job. How much would it cost? The objective is to put the spotlight on the economic value of ecosystem services in, for example, community planning to lend it weight in the decision processes.

Erik Sjödin has long worked with pollinators such as honeybees, wild bees, bumblebees, and butterflies in his artistic practice. In the project *Our Friends the Pollinators,* he has organized workshops where children and young people have built bee hotels to promote the survival of the pollinators. In his work *The Political Beekeeper's Library,* he has compiled

Erik Sjödin, *The Political Beekeeper's Library*, 2015

literary descriptions of bees, many of which refer to bee colonies as metaphors for the forms of government where and when the books were written, from earlier references to the bee as a king or queen in a monarchy to ideas of more decentralized governments. Every writer has been convinced that his or her analysis is correct, but what becomes evident is that it has been possible to apply diametrically opposed metaphors on bee colonies, which perhaps is more of a reflection on the writer than the colonies themselves.

In their work *Forest Law*, Ursula Biemann and Paulo Tavares (p. 153) call attention to the remarkable fact that Ecuador has become the first country in the world to recognize the rights of nature in its constitution. The video installation tells of land conflicts where companies want to exploit natural resources and where the local population is in opposition to it and argue for the rights of nature in a court of law. Witnesses explain that the forest is not just an empty shell; it is alive and populated both by human and nonhuman beings. It is an extraordinary feeling to hear someone refer to the spirits of nature in a court of law, giving the sense that other priorities are possible under the right conditions.

Carolina Caycedo's project *Be Dammed* (2012–ongoing) addresses the consequences of large-scale hydroelectric dams. Most of the works set out from meetings with people who have been affected by hydroelectric dam developments. Sometimes entire rivers are redirected without consideration for either social or natural ecologies. In the project, the artist works with geo-choreographies—political actions that are based on the assumption that geography and territory are part of the body, not something exterior to it. It may be about getting together and reclaiming the right to move in the flood area, manifesting that water is a human right and should be a common good and not a commodity that can be bought and sold. Geo-choreographies may be a method to strengthen people whose interests and needs have been brushed aside by the hydroelectric industry and politicians.

Marjetica Potrč highlights a community in a remote area of the Brazilian part of the Amazonas in works such as the drawing series *Florestania* (p. 101), the text *New Territories in Acre and Why They Matter*,[6] and the architectural study *Xapuri: Rural School*

Ursula Biemann and Paulo Tavares, *Forest Law*, 2014, video still with José Gualingua, leader of the Kichwa people of Sarayaku, Ecuador

Carolina Caycedo, *Águas para a Vida*, 2016, collective action during the 32nd Bienal de São Paulo. "A year of impunity of the social and environmental crime committed by Samarco (Vale/BHP Billiton) in Brasil, we call 'Water Is Life' in solidarity with the affected communities of the Doce River basin," published on Carolina Caycedo's Instagram (@lacaycedo), November 5, 2016

Carolina Caycedo, *Watu, Yaqui, Yuma, Elwha, and Iguacu*, 2016, from the *River Books* series

Carolina Caycedo, *Land of Friends*, 2014

Carolina Caycedo, *YUMA, or the Land of Friends,* 2014; installation view at the 8th Berlin Biennale, 2014

Carolina Caycedo, *Serpent River Book,* 2017

99

(pp. 102–03). The community is geographically isolated but the inhabitants are reaching out on their own terms by using technological solutions. They realize the importance of being a part of the world outside while also protecting their integrity. Keywords for the community are self-organization, sustainable development, and shared knowledge. Grassroot initiatives collaborate with the government, which, among other things, supports the building of schools. The local school is equipped with solar panels to produce electricity and a satellite with which to communicate with the world. The work focuses on grassroot initiatives, which makes the inaccessible forest location into an asset on the road toward sustainable development.

Futurefarmers is an international collective of artists, activists, researchers, farmers, and architects who together initiate, curate, and produce art projects that question our knowledge and suggest new ways of organizing our societies. In the project *Seed Journey* (pp. 104–05), Futurefarmers gathered a number of dedicated researchers, artists, writers, bakers, farmers, and sailors to "save" ancient crops that had fallen into neglect. A voyage in a wooden rescue sailboat from Oslo to Istanbul, with stopovers at nine port cities along the Atlantic and Mediterranean coasts, carried seeds with a dramatic history, such as seeds from the Vavilov Institute's seed bank, which was protected and preserved during the Siege of Leningrad, as well as forgotten seed varieties, which, for example, had been discovered between floor boards, and which people have been able to cultivate, harvest, and share. The project generates new networks along the way and documents the history of the plants while protecting biological diversity and the knowledge about it.

All the artworks in the exhibition fill me with a sense of enthusiasm. None of them offer any ultimate solution to the big problem. But each and every one of them shows that it is possible to do *something,* and that it is possible to think of multiple things simultaneously—the self, surrounding societies, and natural ecologies on a global scale. It is possible to question how mental ecologies are formed and to suggest other orders of priority and ways of looking at the world. It is possible to question how social ecologies are affected by exploitation and to turn vulnerability into strength. It is possible to acknowledge the rights of nature in a way that its cause weighs more than that of large corporations in a court of law. The beginning of a different world is at least possible.

---

1  Félix Guattari, *The Three Ecologies* (London and New York, 2008). First published in 1989.

2  Gregory Bateson, *Steps to an Ecology of Mind* (Chicago, 2000). First published in 1972.

3  Nils-Aslak Valkeapää, "A Way of Calming Reindeer," *Scandinavian Review* 71, no. 2 (June 1983), p. 44.

4  The Intergovernmental Platform for Biodiversity and Ecosystem Services, "Europe and Central Asia Dialogue Workshop on Indigenous and Local Knowledge Systems," (presentation, Paris, January 11–13, 2016).

5  *Working with Nature—Sami Reindeer Herders and Biodiversity in the Boreal Forest,* directed by Samuel Roturier (2016), short film.

6  Marjetica, Potrč, "New Territories in Acre and Why They Matter," *e-flux journal* 00 (2008), http://www.e-flux.com/journal/00/68461/new-territories-in-acre-and-why-they-matter/.

Marjetica Potrč, *Florestania,* 2006–10; in the image, drawing number ten

Marjetica Potrč, *Xapuri: Rural School,* 2006; on the left: source image; on the right: installation view at *How to Live Together*, 27th Bienal de São Paulo, 2006

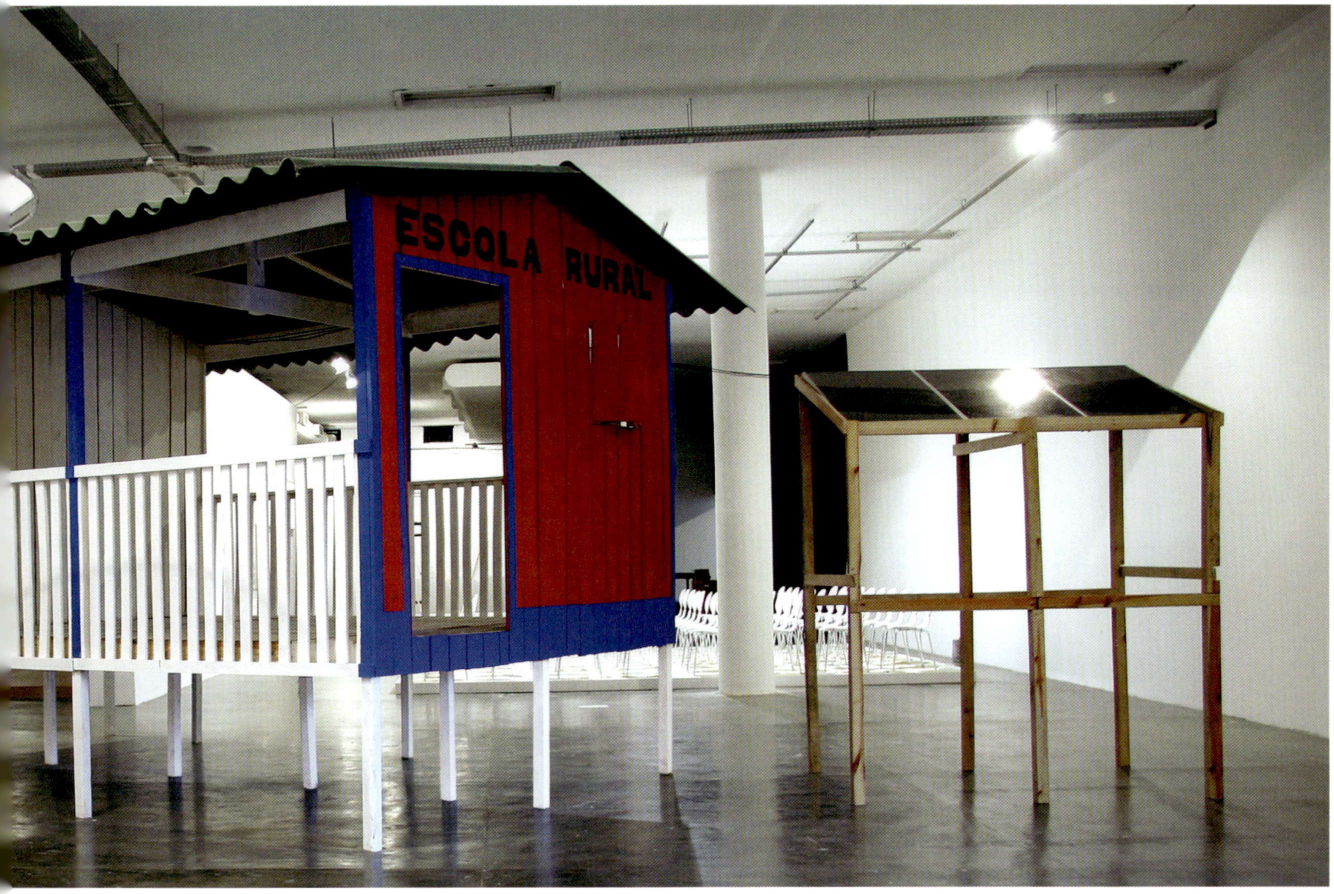
ESCOLA RURAL

Futurefarmers, *Seed Procession,* Oslo, 2016

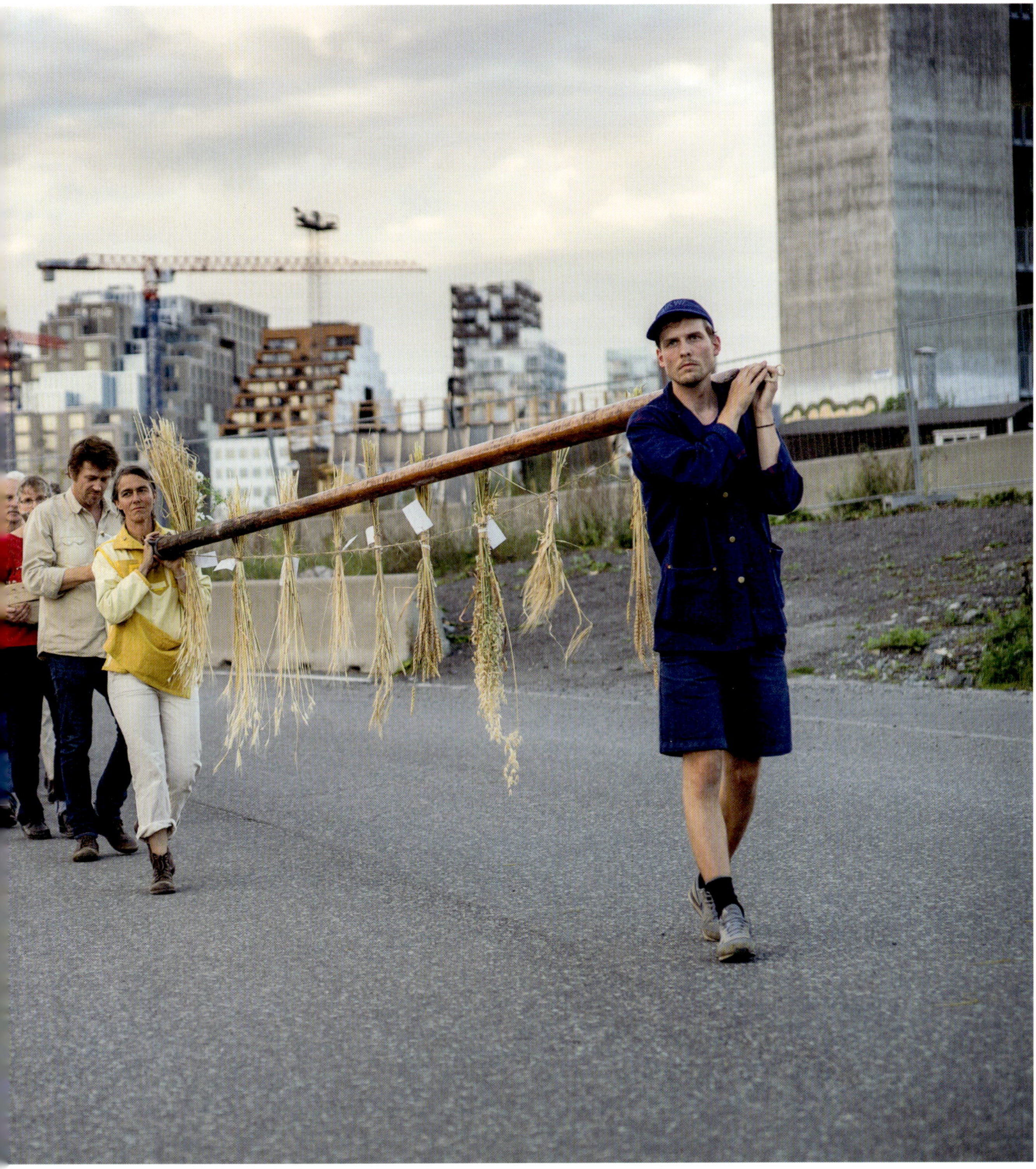

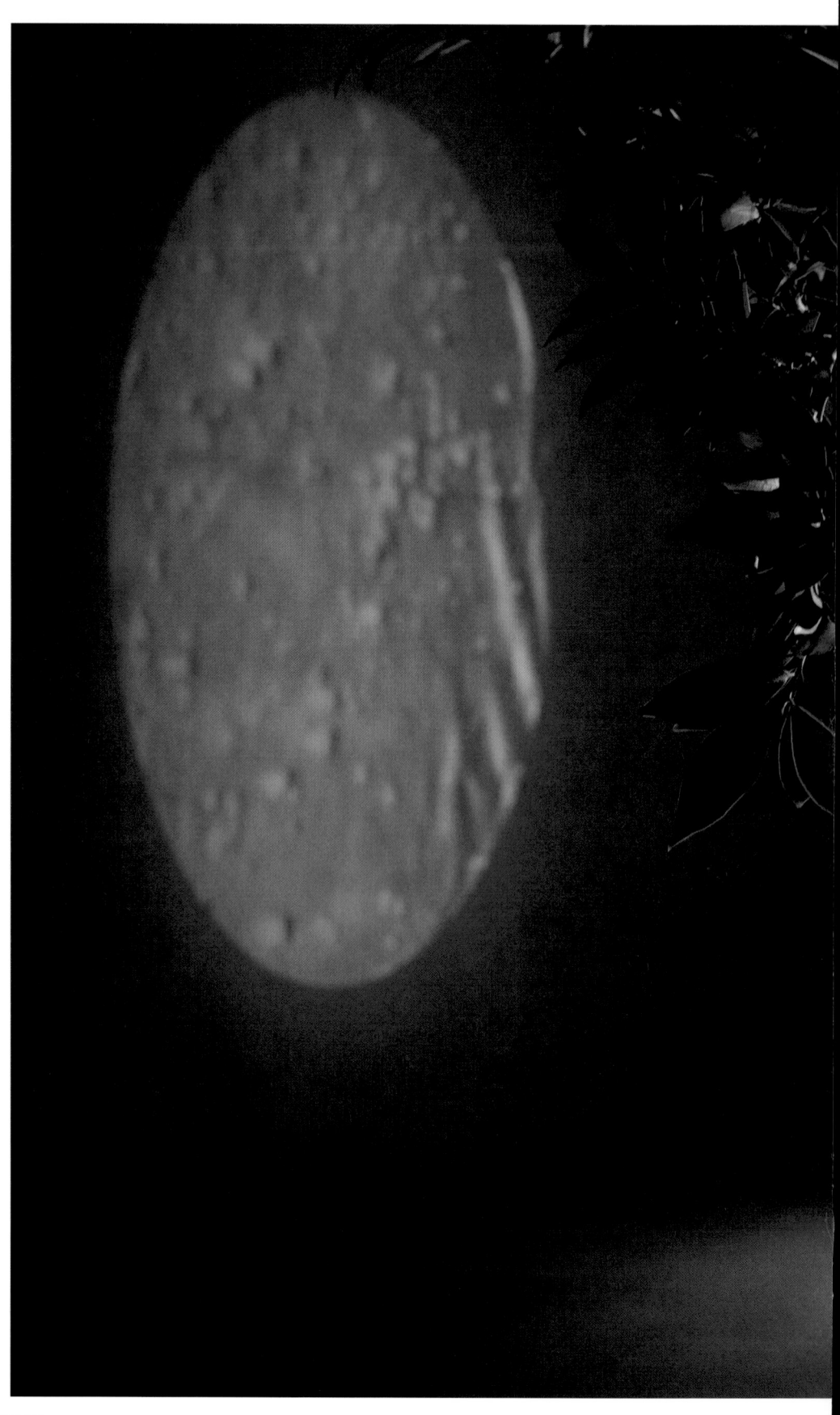

Terike Haapoja, *Inhale-Exhale*, 2008/13

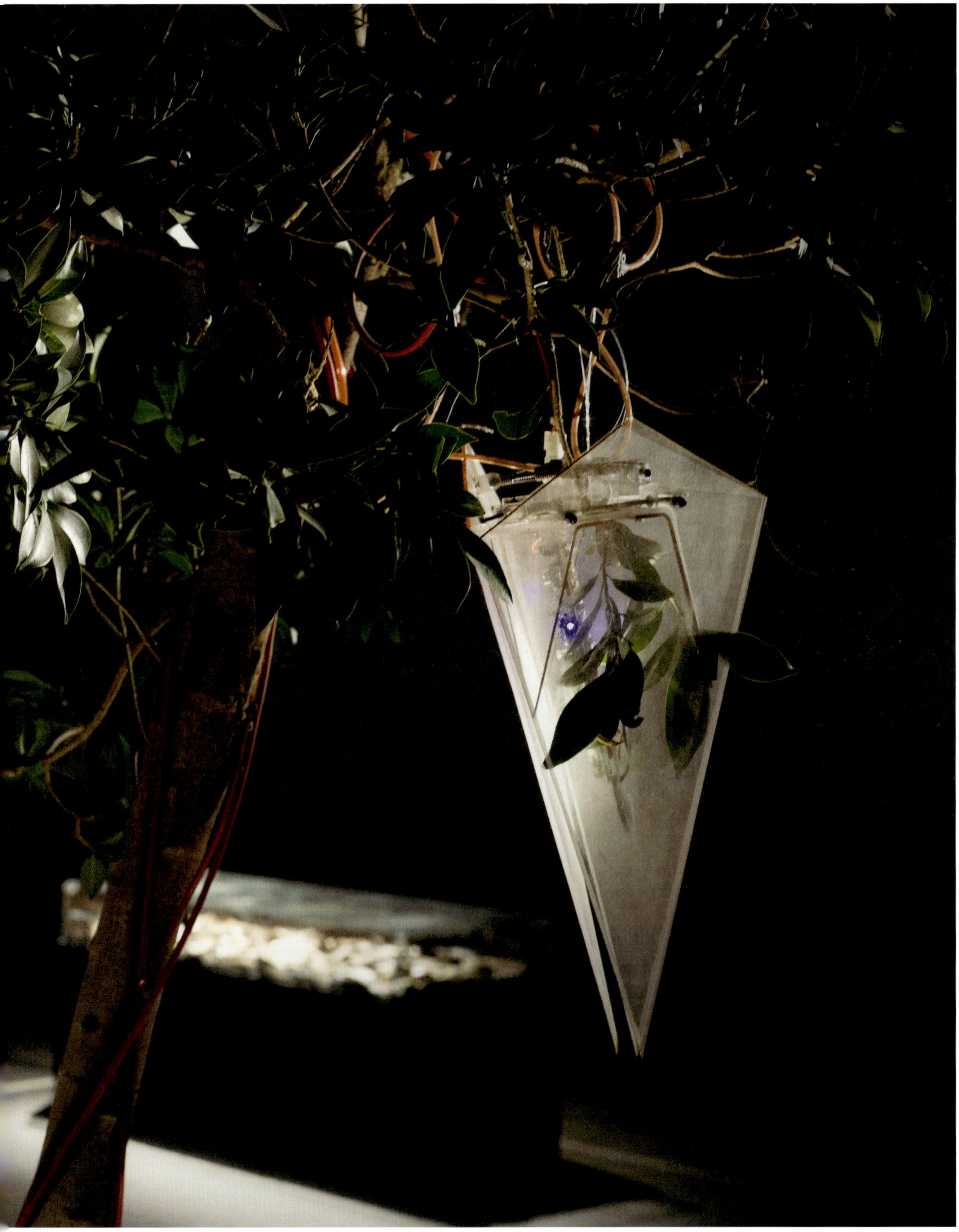

GOOGLE.COM EMITTED **12638.43** KG OF CO2 SINCE YOU OPENED THIS PAGE

Joana Moll, *CO2GLE*, 2014

Joana Moll, *DEFOOOOOOOOOOOOOOOOOOOOOREST*, 2016

# ECODATA—ECOMEDIA—ECO-AESTHETICS: TECHNOLOGIES OF THE ECOLOGICAL AFTER THE ANTHROPOCENE

YVONNE VOLKART,[1]
IN COOPERATION WITH KARIN OHLENSCHLÄGER
AND SABINE HIMMELSBACH

"If media can make a difference in investigating the ecological crisis, we need to begin with media technology itself."[2]

In the arts, the impression has been created for some years that the concepts "Anthropocene," "Capitalocene," and "technosphere" have outranked ecological or green ideas. The notion that we earthlings are stuck in a machine that has gotten out of control has an iron grip on us. But can we counter this apocalypse with something by "sharing" the newest photos from our cell phones? And what good does it do if I change my life when Africa is being hollowed out on a massive scale and filled up with electronic waste? How can visions develop when ecological or green thinking has migrated to the inflationary language of supermarkets and corporations in such a way that it then simply seems arbitrary, unsexy, or neoliberal?

Gilberto Esparza, *BioSoNot 2.0*, 2017

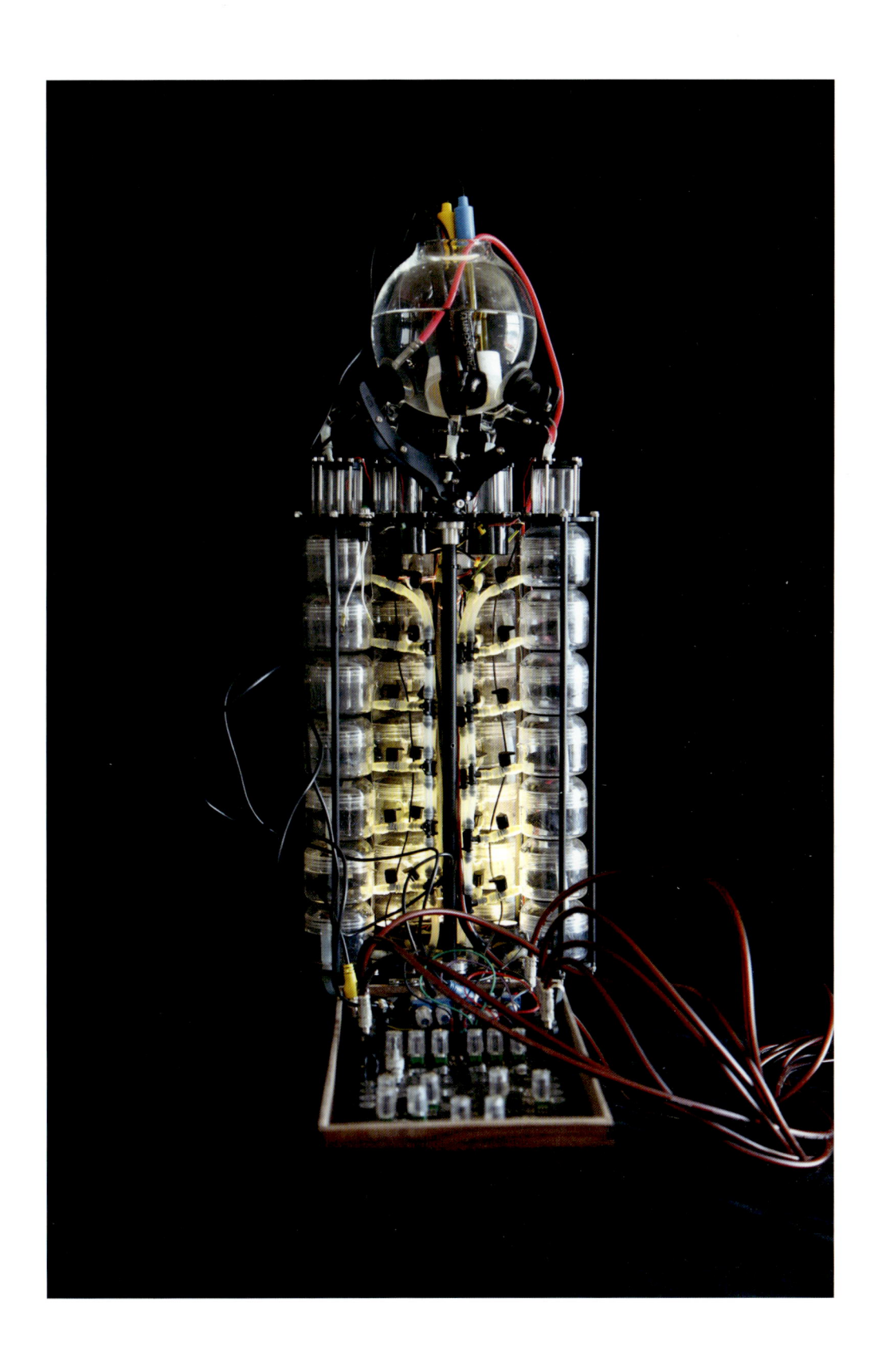

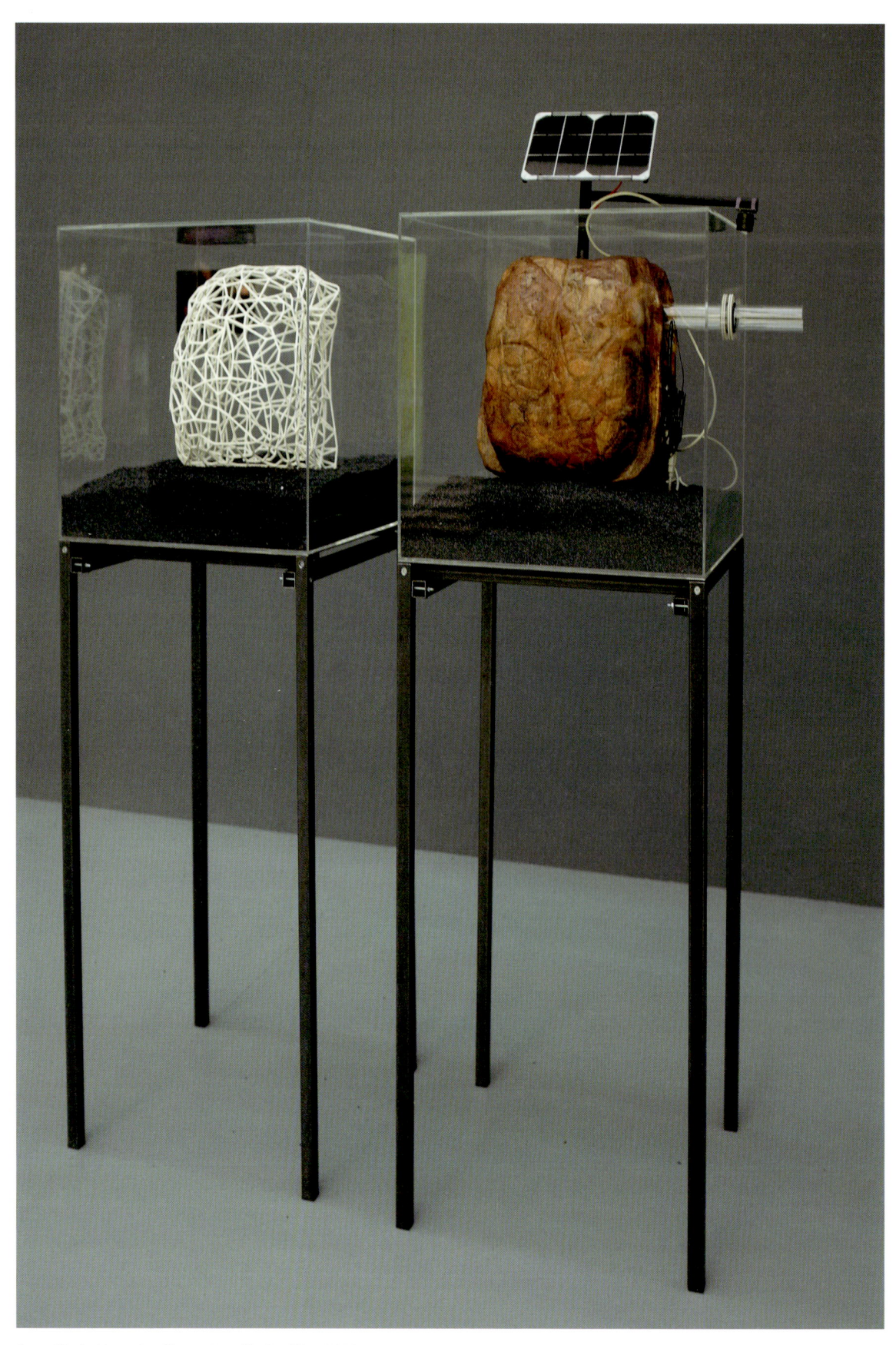

Anne Marie Maes, *Intelligent Guerilla Beehive*, 2016

As well-conditioned machine subjects of this machine world, we know that we have hardly any other choice than to accept the contradictions: we abhor the exploitation of the Global South and are nonetheless involved in it as accomplices. If we would like to contribute something productive to the current situation, we have to accept our imperfectness with all humility and perhaps also with a bit of humor. (And why not post pictures of my compost worms on Instagram?) It is necessary to develop eco-aesthetic, transversal thought and action that recognizes our paradoxical and corrupted form of existence, and opens up other levels instead of simply offering simple technical "solutions" or dismissing the technological as something alien to our nature. This means leaving the Anthropocene behind and trying to open up prospects of an "after the Anthropocene"—of an "afterlife" in the here and now.

For this reason, we have chosen to continue to use the term "eco," because it has potential. Also, counter to those who maintain that ecological or green thinking is characterized as too harmonic (deep ecology, Gaia) or dualistic (we have to save nature), recognizing the biosphere as an *oikos* (household), which means differentiated relationships between various protagonists and their "niches," does not necessarily have to signify harmony. It instead recognizes that things and living beings are embedded in quite specific relational, hence interconnected, relationships. These "network ecologies" (Jennifer Gabrys) are not always obvious to others. Hence, thinking ecologically means examining all the chains, correlations, processes, dependencies, conditions, and interfaces in which the very diverse animate and inanimate inhabitants of the earth "coexist" (Timothy Morton). The environment, the surrounding world, is no longer what is external to the human animal, no longer "nature"; it is instead "our" bio-technosphere, which we share, inhabit together, and therefore also engender. It is now necessary to work on this understanding of our world as a "commons" since the economic perspective that regards everything outside of its interests as passively given, devaluing and turning it into waste, is far too dominant. The involvement of artists today therefore consists to a great extent of sensitizing us to what we occupy and destroy out of ignorance or complicity. Media technologies and interdisciplinary cooperation with the natural and techno-sciences play a substantial role in this and challenge conventional concepts of art. In what follows, we would like to discuss the spectrum of ecomedia strategies and visionary positions from our exhibition.

**ECOMEDIA AS INSTRUMENTS FOR INCREASING ATTENTION**

In the touring exhibition *Ecomedia* (2007–09) we started to become interested in the question of how artists make use of media and technologies in exploring the ecological, media technologies that we seem to use so confidently, while they—and their automatisms or the service providers coupled with them—use us as well. We understood these technologies not only as instruments, but frequently also as fractured and paradoxical actors. They are involved so ubiquitously and powerfully in producing knowledge about our biosphere that one can actually no longer get around not appropriating, alienating, or "abstracting" them. We called them ecomedia. Similar terms are geomedia, earth media, and environmental media. Their use gives rise to hybrid conjunctions, between technologies for recording and sending media and the material world and environment (atmosphere, bodies of water, soil, people). Various surveillance technologies as well as data collected by means of various measuring techniques are supposed to facilitate an "articulation" of hitherto unknown worlds and environments in the

Aline Veillat, *Pas de deux en vert et contre*, 2009–12

Joaquín Fargas, *Glaciator*, 2017

form of artifactual media arrangements. The signals received by machines via various methods (e.g. sonification) are frequently also put into a pitch that is audible for human beings. Ecomedia techniques couple us techno-aesthetically with realities about which we (as yet) know nothing, and consequently become mediators between worlds. This is virtual reality of another kind: the perception of a reality that has always already existed virtually. Ecomedia thus function in real life and symbolically as instruments for increasing attention with respect to nonhuman protagonists.

While information technologies record changes on planet earth and transform it into "Program Earth,"[3] natural scientists understand the zones of "nature" that they observe in an especially systematic way as outdoor laboratories.[4] Karen Barad speaks of the fact that people experiment with the earth because they do not know what effects their (technology-based) actions have.

This technologically generated ontological status of the earth as a machine, program, laboratory, and experiment with an unforeseeable outcome has prompted us to inquire—more specifically within the framework of the current exhibition *Eco–Visionaries* than in the exhibition *Ecomedia*—into the significance and aesthetics of data, technologies, and methods of the natural sciences in art: what do media technologies accomplish with respect to sensitizing the public to ecology? What aesthetic settings, narratives, and experiences do they engender? How do they deal with or disrupt techno-natural scientific methods? Are there new forms of intimacy (between bodies, technologies, and data), of communication, emotion, and the transgression (of species), and what does this mean with reference to the human ability to act?

These questions interest us not only because media artists experiment particularly intensely with hybrid, artifactual, and transmedial arrangements, or strive to make their access to the experience of the world a subject of discussion. What seems to be linked to media technologies is, indeed, the (positivistic) hope that an environmental problem then—when it can be substantiated with data—becomes something of which people are generally aware and can be altered. Trends in the direction of citizen science projects, i.e. also collecting environmental data outside the arts, substantiate this. In our opinion, however, in the case of these techno-cultural practices it is more a question of participation and emotional involvement than of obtaining information. Because does the problem not really consist in the fact that we very often have the information (about high levels of air pollution, etc.), but ultimately do not do anything with it?[5] Because it would be inconvenient? Because it would mean openly saying no to whitewashing? Is not what we need instead a different kind of information and other ways of obtaining it? A being-involved, a surplus of information that we perceive with the senses, that moves us aesthetically and hence gives us the courage to say no?

> "[S]atellites are to ecological activism what cellphone cameras are to #BlackLivesMatter…. When the cool, abstract data of the environmental sciences are adopted and expressed by impassioned individuals and groups, you get the Climate Justice Movement. Spanning the globe with its powerful proxies, the climate movement turns data into knowledge, then it turns knowledge into aesthetic forms, and finally it turns aesthetic forms into action."[6]

Rasa Smite & Raitis Smits, *Fluctuations of Microworlds*, 2017

Chris Jordan, *Albatross,* 2017, video still

Brian Holmes's argumentation is exemplary for the assumptions that are widespread among many activism-oriented media artists and theorists: that the tools practically turn us into activists automatically. In reality, however, the crux, which neither technologies nor art, nor other nonhuman stakeholders can resolve, lies precisely in the leap from knowledge to action. Needed at this point are simply also, as Félix Guattari emphasized, groups of people who do so.[7] The hope in art, as a result of its ability to involve people emotionally and mobilize them, at least on the level of the senses, is nevertheless not unfounded: people who have seen an albatross die on film and in front of a camera will very likely have a different relationship to birds, plastic, and perhaps also to activism than beforehand.

We maintain that the visionary and moving quality of artistic projects lies in producing an aesthetic surplus. In other words: the visionary potential of ecological art lies not only in addressing exploitative relationships in terms of content or in outlining utopian fantasies and counter-models, but also in generating unexpected aesthetic experiences with our co-beings.

**FROM RECORDING DATA TO GENERATING RELATIONAL COMMUNICATION AND LIFE MODELS**

Ecomedia strategies have shifted in the past ten years: while recording and interpreting in the form of visualizing/sonicating relatively clearly defined objects, such as weather data, once stood in the foreground, the new technologies today intervene directly in ecosystems. The latter are perceived in their material vibrancy, techno-organic artifactuality, and indeterminability. In this sense, technologies monitor or track nonhuman, seemingly "insignificant" small protagonists, such as bees, ants, or worms, so as to make it possible to experience their being as singular modes of existence within a comprehensive context.

We would like to highlight the following strategies:

A fundamental method of ecological thinking today comprises showing linkages between the protagonists and things involved, and making the technological as well as economic and milieu-based dependencies and/or relations of exploitation comprehensible. What is new in this is the specific focus on the suppressed and in part seemingly apocalyptic flip side of our data and trash society. This is represented in the net art projects *DEFOOOOOOOOOOOOO-OOOOOOOOOREST* and *CO2GLE* by the Spanish artist Joana Moll (pp. 108–09), the *Unravelled* (pp. 128–29) project by the British artist collective Unknown Fields Division, and the video *Albatross* by the American Chris Jordan.

One central means that provides evidence of previously unknown functional processes in the microcellular field, and also serves as a means of sensitizing and exciting people about other levels of reality, is the use of sound within the framework of acoustic ecology. This includes the apparatus *BioSoNot 2.0* (p. 111) by the Mexican artist Gilberto Esparza, the installation *treelab* (pp. 122–23) by the Swiss artist Marcus Maeder, and the work *Reserva Sonora de la Biosfera de Asturias* (pp. 162–63) by the Spanish sound artist Juanjo Palacios.

Not sound, but instead interactive apparatuses or "prostheses" can become an aesthetic means for making the behavior of particular ecosystems or protagonists visible, such as plants.

This strategy is in operation in the installations *Inhale-Exhale* (pp. 106–07) and *Dialogue* (p. 125) by the Finnish artist Terike Haapoja as well as in the installation *Pas de deux en vert et contre* (p. 114) by the French artist Aline Veillat.

Sensor-supported recording, monitoring, and experimenting with living microsystems, as well as translating them into extensive transmedial installations, is the method used in *Fluctuations of Microworlds* (p. 117) by the Latvian artist duo Rasa Smite & Raitis Smits, and in *Intelligent Guerilla Beehive* (p. 112) by the Belgian artist Anne Marie Maes.

More and more artists are working within the framework of symbiotic, experimental, and laboratory-like practices that interweave human and nonhuman, and artifactual protagonists, milieus, and machines, in surprising relationships. They are made possible by experiments, communication, emotions, and empathy. This is done by the Swiss artist duo Baggenstos/Rudolf with their installation *Fostering Duckweed—From Urine to Protein*, and by knowbotiq's *Genesis Machine* (p. 136) as well as the wearable *Symbiotic Interaction* (pp. 126–27) by the Spanish artist couple María Castellanos and Alberto Valverde.

The empirical knowledge of the Anthropocene that the earth is a planet with limited resources and is construed as an experimental laboratory, both materially and digitally, is addressed in the installation *Domestic Catastrophe N° 3: La Planète Laboratoire* (pp. 166–67) by the French artist duo HeHe. The five-channel video installation *Earthworks* (pp. 28–29) by the British artist duo Semiconductor and *Glaciator* (p. 115) by the Argentinian artist Joaquín Fargas also move in this direction.

Artistic visions in the period of the Anthropocene are difficult. They can all too easily become infected by either the technocracy that makes large-scale projects such as geoengineering so repelling, or by that kind of salvation thinking that we are familiar with from diverse religions. Visions, if they do not want to be simple or spiritual means for solutions, can always only be experienced aesthetically or sketched out by means of multiple refracted patterns and figurations. The performative video installation *Acoustic Ocean* (pp. 146–47) by the Swiss artist Ursula Biemann attempts to do this by introducing a charismatic figure that mediates between water and land, knowledge and action—and hence by opening up a sort of fictitious path on which we earthlings might set forth, together.

---

1   Research project funded by the Swiss National Science Foundation.

2   Richard Maxwell et.al., "Introduction," in *Media and the Ecological Crisis,* ed. Richard Maxwell et al. (New York and London, 2014).

3   Jennifer Gabrys, *Program Earth: Environmental Sensing Technology and the Making of a Computational Planet* (Minneapolis and London, 2016).

4   Andreas Rigling in discussion with the author, Swiss Federal Institute for Forest, Snow, and Landscape Research, WSL, August 2017.

5   Naturally, there are many nations that manipulate publically accessible measurement data, such as Japan, for example, does for radioactivity in the ground. This is why alternative or activist measuring cultures have established themselves. In Switzerland, where the relevance of data is not a problem, the danger is simply glossed over so that it is possible to raise the maximum values, as is currently being done for the levels of pesticides in bodies of water.

6   Brian Holmes, "Empathiemaschinen: Neue Organe für den Ökokörper?" *Springerin* 4 (2017), p. 28.

7   Félix Guattari, "Remaking Social Practices," in *The Guattari Reader,* ed. Gary Genosko (Oxford, 1996), p. 262–72.

8   The other artists of this video installation are Mark Hansen, Laura Kurgan, and Ben Rubin, in collaboration with Robert Gerard Pietrusko and Stewart Smith. It is based on an idea by Paul Virilio.

Baggenstos/Rudolf, *Fostering Duckweed—From Urine to Protein*, 2016–17

Marcus Maeder, *treelab*, 2017

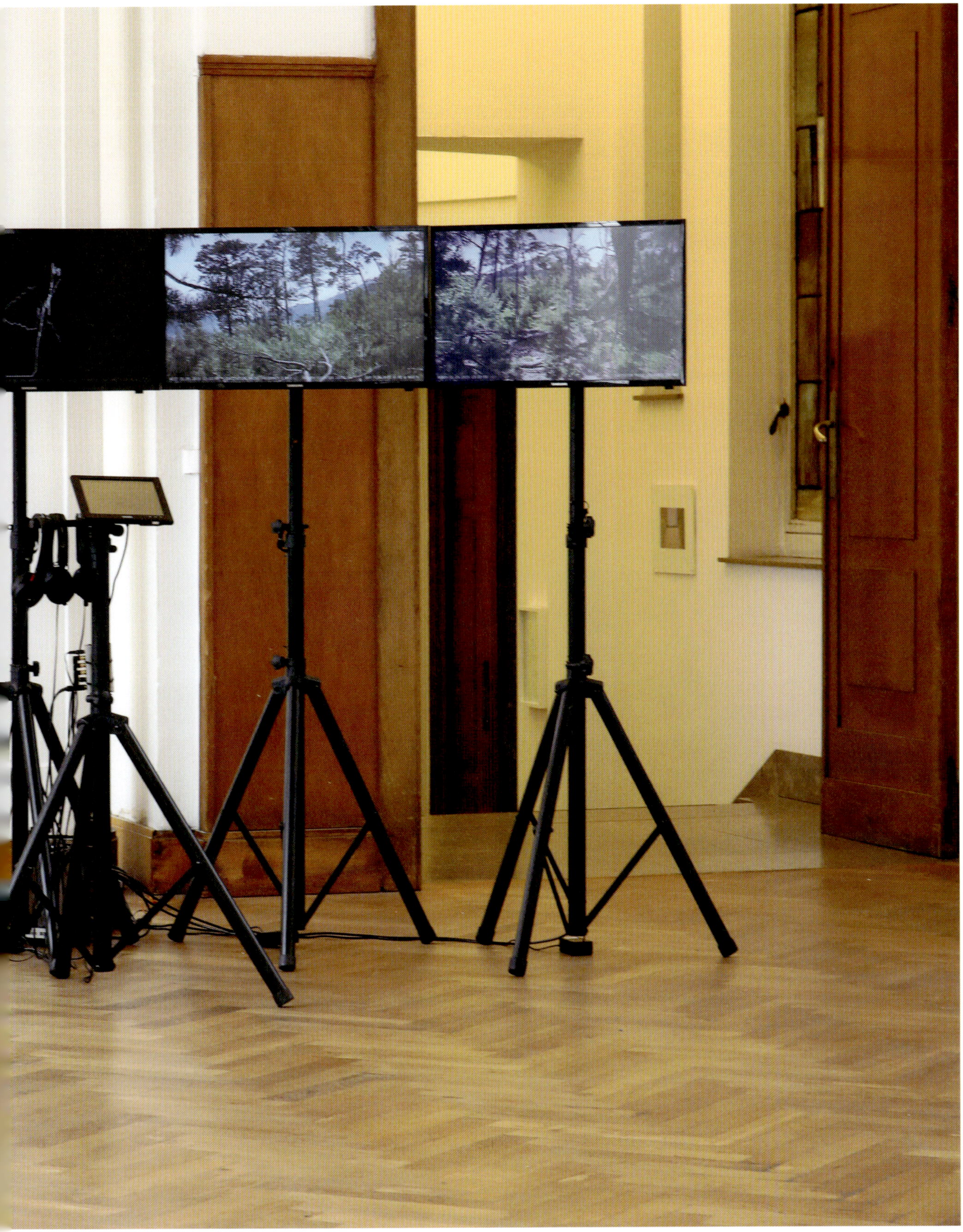

Terike Haapoja, *Dialogue,* 2008

María Castellanos and Alberto Valverde, *Symbiotic Interaction,* 2017

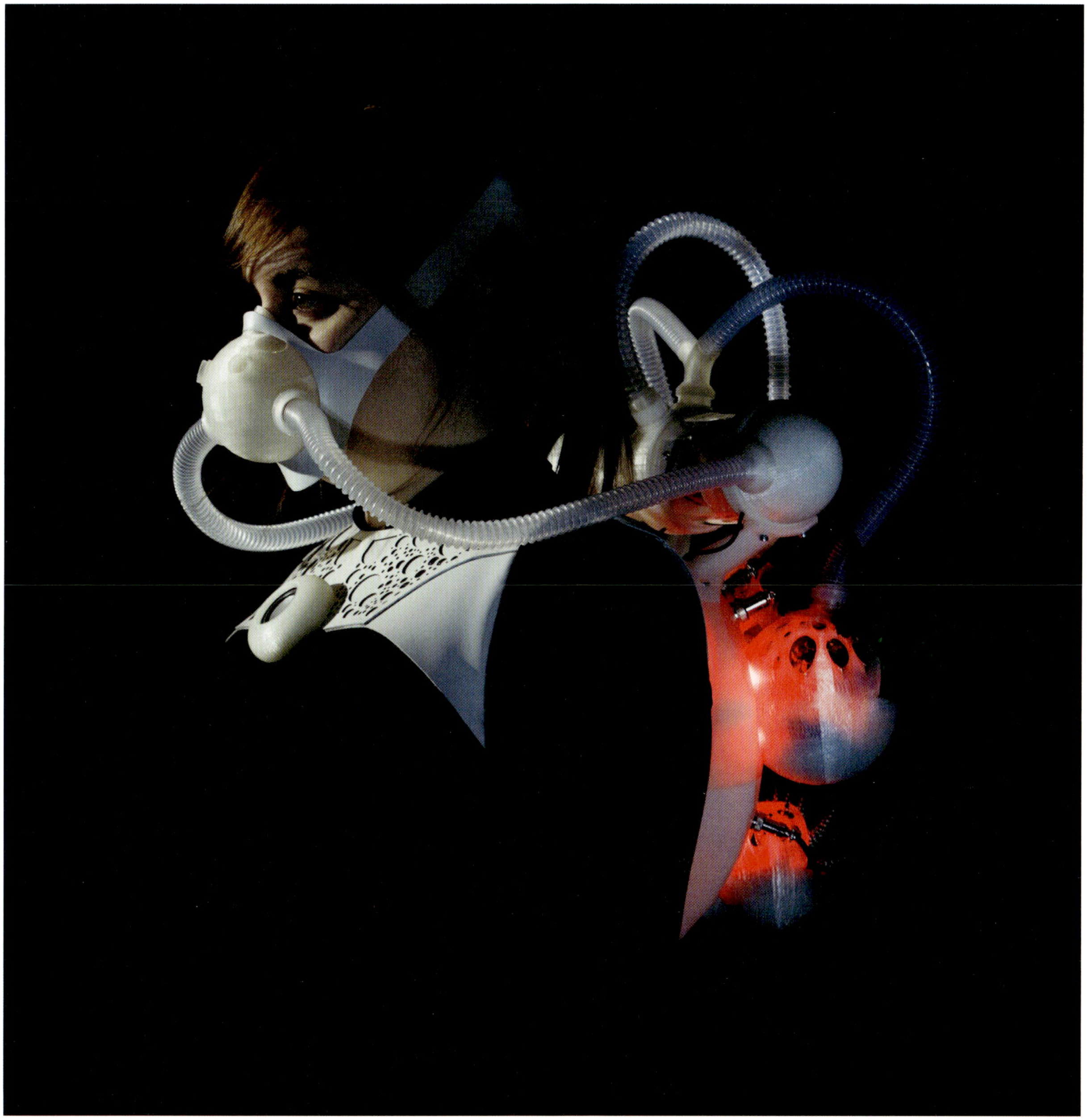

Unknown Fields Division, *Unravelled,* 2017

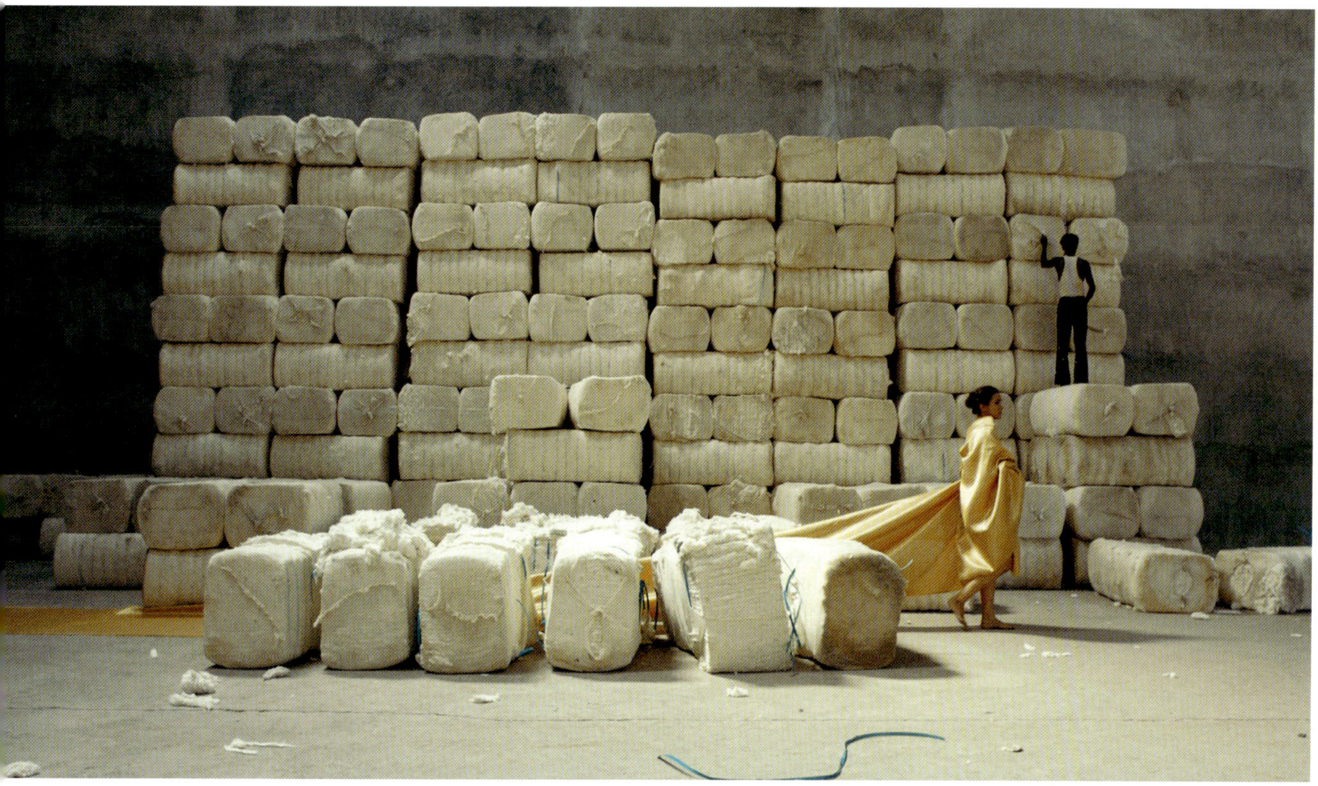

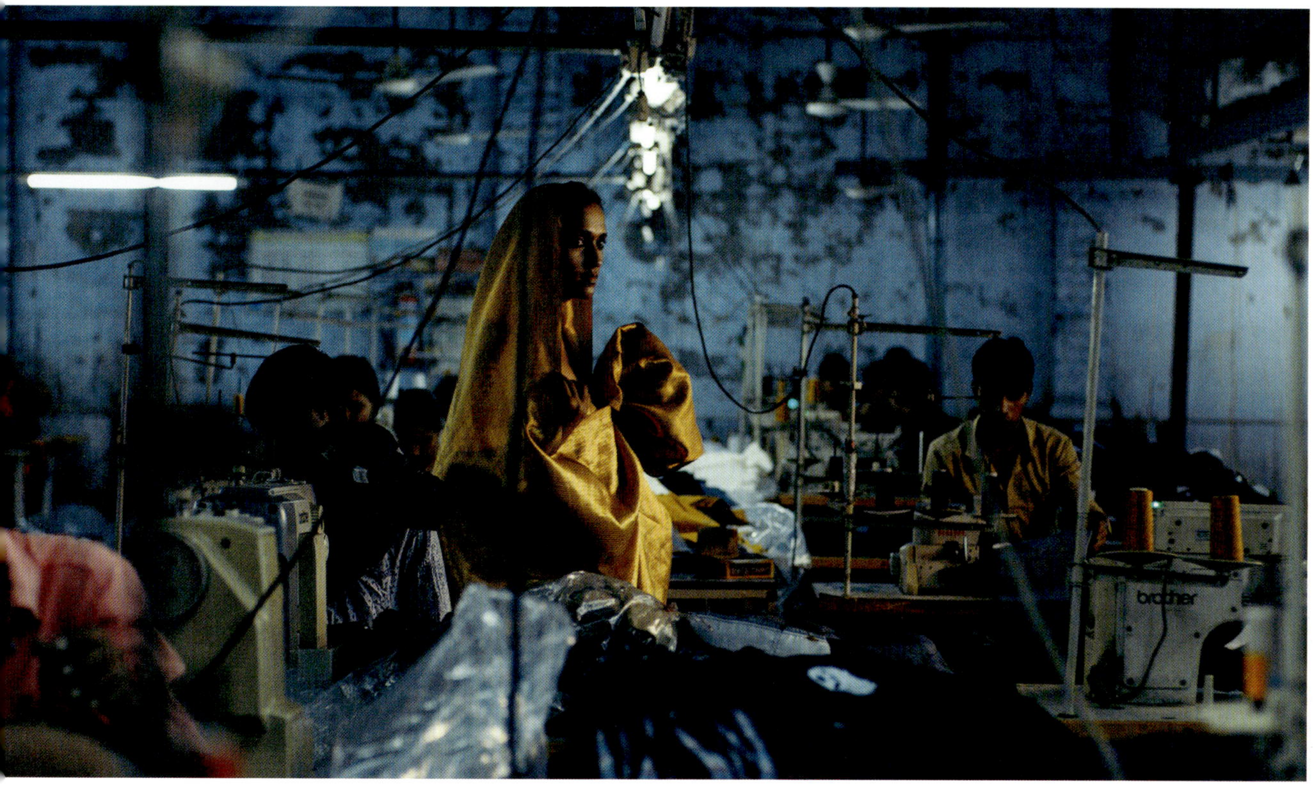
brother

# FIGURING ECOLOGIES

*MATTHEW FULLER*

Over the course of the last century or so, the study of ecologies moved from their description to their analysis. Broad catalogues and narrations of landscapes and species, sometimes expressed in the terms of colonial wonder and avarice, were supplemented by attempts to finely understand the interactions and dependencies of things such as species and systems. In the present, as the fragility of the conditions that have historically lasted up until the industrial epoch begin to be recognized, ecological practices, in their conceptual and scientific dimensions, now move from analysis, a term which implies a certain separation (expressed positively as disinterestedness, neutrality), to an understanding that more readily includes an embeddedness and contingency. The understanding of this embeddedness is both claustrophobic and empowering of experimental forms of life. It is claustrophobic since it seems that, at present, there is only this specimen of a planet, and living in peace and equality upon it seems to be rather difficult for the dominant species. It empowers experiment since once the implied distanciation of analysis is rendered equivocal, if locally stabilizable and necessary, forms of reflexivity are implied that draw the experimenter into a dance and a dialogue with the materials, conditions, models, and crises worked with. Here, analysis comes into its own in a complex form in which it is not distanciated from the world, but drawn into its composition. The argument in this article is that it is in part the particular qualities of mathematics as a medium of thought and knowledge, generalized into computational systems for understanding ecologies, that provide some of the texture of this condition.

This experimental phase includes an experimentation of the worst: the brinksmanship of climate damage, the flooding of seas with plastics, the use of mortifying chemicals on crops and creatures. The cutting of corners and the offloading of costs as externalities are only a few of the terms by which this mode of experimentalism operates. It also includes currents

Regina Frank—The HeArt is Present, *ILand (in sickness in health)*, 2018

Pedro Neves Marques, *The Pudic Relation Between Machine and Plant*, 2016

in which the tools of physicists migrate to the metaphysics of financialization, and abstract machines developed to analyze the composition of the cosmos are mobilized to act on that of populations, disciplining and eliciting behaviors.

The humans' peculiar condition of simultaneously being an as yet relatively undomesticated animal, a creature of civilizations (a political animal, in Aristotle's term), and an object of its own invention (the posthuman, as Rosi Braidotti describes it[1]) plays a part in this sense of embeddedness, but it is also traceable through the expansion of the capacity, indeed the necessity, in computing—now our fundamental media of knowledge—to carry out calculations on calculations. One route into ecological embeddedness is thus via abstraction, but this can also be a thick abstraction, rich with its own textures and dilemmas; not one that always pretends to reduce the universe to the simple roll-out of a set of mechanical laws, but one that plays with, in both ambiguous senses of the term, the kelp, whales, and plasmodium, the bacteria, formulas, and atmosphere that make this world.

One passage into this condition is to trace the role of information as a framework for understanding ecology. Information theory, developed by Claude E. Shannon and Warren Weaver, has been essential to the understanding of systems and of ecologies as assemblages of systems.[2] But it is sometimes used mechanistically, as a form of gross reduction.[3] Much of the contemporary understanding of ecology relies on information, and information is also something that, through a certain set of lenses, is produced in and by ecological entities. A stimulus on the surface of a membrane, such as the movement of a chemical across a tongue, the translation of such an event to a neural signal, or the release of saliva as a response to that signal, might all count as being informational; as might, at a certain resolution of analysis, the interaction of species—perhaps coevolving predator and prey—in a habitat; or the space of possible permutations within what is described as a species, or what, under the conditions of information, is understood as being *encoded* in a gene. Necessarily, in the condition of being regarded as informational, there is a translation of values obtained empirically towards their expression via mathematical means. As well as understanding the losses, gains, and problems associated with such a translation as it maps entities in the world in relation to number, there are other textures arising within systems of number themselves that come into play; and it is these that I want to look at first before returning to the question of the texture of wider ecologies as they partially mix with them.

**NUMBERS AMONGST NUMBERS**

The mathematical genealogy of the theory of information suggests a means of understanding such textures of experimental embeddedness. One could start this narrative at a number of points at which the use of enumeration and of calculation elicits new capacities and understandings of matter. The inventions of geometry and of calculus would be such points of inflection, in which relations between systems of measurement and between measurements, calculation, and abstraction generate particular kinds of consistency. Where we can also trace a relation to ecology is through the action of numbers and procedures on other numbers and systems of numbering. Mathematics here becomes a highly recursive and inventive process. We can say that several mathematicians at the beginning of the twentieth century provided grounds for a diagonal thinking. All these works are partially concerned with the internal constraints to mathematics and to logic as regards their ability to self-describe. Here, modern mathematics adopts highly formal procedures that, in variant form, would be taken up later by artists and poets in conceptual and post-conceptual art, but that also lay the ground for critical and reflexive practices with other kinds of materials.

Linguistic and enumerative forms produce moiré patterns of interference between one disciplinary formalization and another in an ecology of symbols, conceptual forces, and meanings. These moiré patterns in turn offer their distinct qualities and limitations as means of understanding the world. Georg Cantor's 1891 formulation of the "diagonal method" is notable here in that, when laid out in a table or in a line, in other words in any formal structure, an additional number "in-between" other numbers can always be found or made. (For instance between 0.1 and 0.2 is 0.15 and a continuous myriad of other numbers.) Here, discreteness and infinity co-exist, and a flickering between them is inherent to this system of enumeration. Analysis is texturally predisposed to paradox. It is in working with the world, with empirical data of various kinds, with contexts that demand attentive rigor, that experimentality and embeddedness are lent versions of their powers. In a later intervention, that provided much of the grounds for information theory, Kurt Gödel's incompleteness theorem shows that there are interdependencies in systems of enumeration; complex hierarchies of reflexivity that establish what is or is not describable at a particular scale. These echo, but are not the same as, those in ecologies.[4] It is their difference that makes them readily useful for understanding each other.

The paradoxes of enumerative power are a way of inducing perception to shed its habitual loads, to see the shimmer of alternate realities in the formation of life. In certain readings, one can see that there is a difference, in that the paradox never fully resolves or resolves on a higher level of abstraction, or in the recognition of the absence of the possibility for such.[5] The historian of mathematics Jeremy Gray describes this moment as a "great liberation" for mathematicians (releasing them from the iron claw of formalism).[6] It is such freedom, textured by paradoxes, but also run through with immense capacities for synthesis, that requires mathematics to be constructivist, to be inventive, rather than to simply annotate precious glimpses of the imagined eternal verities or ideals, which earlier formulations of mathematics, such as those of Plato, offered.

This synthetic constructivism means that mathematics creates its own forms and capacities. These leak out into culture more broadly, but also come into combination with those things that are addressed by mathematical and informational means. Particular forms of computing establish this leakage and recomposition. They texture understandings and syntheses of ecologies through an enormous range of means: sensors, mathematical and logical forms of differentiation between what falls into one category or another; and coding systems, the capacities or languages, databases, algorithms, and logics to deal with the materials garnered and to be worked with. But they are also fundamentally articulated through the ways in which numerical and informational forms of understanding both parse matter and pass into the terms of their composition. The broad range of techniques of genetic engineering would be a prime example of such a condition.

Femke Herregraven, *Sprawling Swamps,* 2016

knowbotiq, *Genesis Machines: La Pompa Agricultura Transsubstantiata*, 2018

In such a formation, there is a fundamental change in the nature of relations between things and the understanding of those things, by the ways in which numbers and the axioms and codes arranging their relations are brought into proximity, indeed are rendered immanent to, the entities that they provide quantities and relations to, as they bring them into or map their composition. Brian Massumi describes computational and digital media's immense "power of their systematization of the possible"[7] as its defining characteristic.

**NUMBERS AMONGST ECOLOGIES**

In 1843, Ada Lovelace noted that the Analytical Engine, a mechanical computer that she and Charles Babbage worked on together, might use mathematical symbols to work on all symbol-based systems, such as musical notation. This would be a form of transcoding, the operation of one code upon another and the use of symbols of one to stand in for that of another. Lovelace and Babbage did not follow this thread up, being consumed by the difficulties of the project itself. The transcoding of media, however, entails the transcoding of number as media and the ability of mathematical forms to act recursively, but non-holistically, upon each other.

This conjunction produces an immense array of actual and potential new practices and figurations of action. The modeling of ecological systems, for instance those of weather or water, starts to feed into the possibility of producing technologies that are both sensitive to such systems and that are able to adjust their relations to them, triggering further differential action. Monitoring and modifying such things as climate or water flows may produce images and fantasies of new kinds of homeostasis, but in turn need to pass through billions of entities across numerous scales and kinds in order to do so. Each of these scales and kinds will impose their own constraints upon those of enumeration and calculation. One of the most significant pieces of information such systems will give to those working with them is the imperative to stay attentive and to be humble. Their particular kinds of unpredictability, as well as their characteristic patterns, those of ecologies, impose a new rigor and potential for diagonal thinking and invention.

Such diagonal thinking has certain ecological characteristics in and of itself. In an environment, numerous organisms and their sub-systems are, at various tempos, competing for and collaborating on the arrangement of resources, nutrients, and reproduction, and are adopting patterns of mutuality, predation, and avoidance. Working into or adapting niches and opportunities, they also communicate, or find the luck to "hijack" or countervail the communications of others. These communications may be chemical, sonic, behavioral, linguistic, and otherwise. Fields such as zoosemiotics and biosemiotics arise in order to trace and experiment with the parameters of such conditions.[8] Further, figuring out the lay of the world via experiment and the reflexive re-arrangement of given orderings is not only a matter of homing in on the most tightly orchestrated execution of an organismic function. It may also be one of evolutionary exuberance at multiple scales[9] and of play at others.[10]

Tracing the diagonal or the emergence of new formations and compositions via the polymorphous nature of the space brought into being by an achieved state of evolution, or via the combinatorial possibilities arranged at the scale of a genotype, phenotype, carbon cycle, food web, or other scale characteristic of biology and ecology, is core to understanding the plenitude of life, but also to investigating the conditions tending towards ecological devastations.[11] Something akin to this diagonal, in that it implies a multi-scalar and exploratory approach to recomposition, is undergone in a bodily and experiential manner by billions of organisms across the earth as they undergo migration and the search of and adaption to new habitats.[12] Further, these movements and experiments change the conditions of being and hence entail recursive cycles of experiment and the drawing out of capacities or constraints in ecosystems. Searching for the ways in which "alternative stable states" outside of historically established patterns may be arrived at, by attending to and making space for, indeed giving into, the ways in which this exploration may be happening, is crucial to humans learning to live well, to investigate, and to struggle in the space of a myriad of recompositions and devastations. In the slipstream of stable states, as they are assembled and maintained by the work of the ecological myriads, is the genesis of novel modalities of information.

The ecologies of numbers amongst numbers and of numbers as a means of the translation and ideation of dynamics occurring in other kinds of material formation may perhaps be believed to begin to cross-fertilize in certain domains. Some of these will bear characteristics reminiscent of the insoluble problems and crises that laid the grounds for the crises of calculation that led to the ideas and techniques of information. Rather than pose ecology as a new, and flattening, universalism, they may lead to the recognition of novel kinds of embeddedness and suggest further wonders in the interstices of the finite.

---

1 Rosi Braidotti, *The Posthuman* (Cambridge, 2013).

2 Claude E. Shannon and Warren Weaver, *The Mathematical Theory of Communication* (Champaign, 1963).

3 Reduction has two meanings, the first is that of reducing a seemingly disparate set of problems or questions to a more singular underlying question through a process of clarification. The second is that of a diminution, the curtailing of the expressiveness of a problem, to something simplistic rather than simple. The former is a matter of scientific labor and intellectual brilliance, the latter is one of short-cuts and of dogma posing as rigor.

4 Kurt Gödel, "Über formal unentscheidbare Sätze der Principia Mathematica und verwandter Systeme, I," in *Collected Works,* vol. I: *Publications 1929–1936,* ed. Solomon Fefermann (Oxford, 1986), pp. 144–95. (Dual German-English text.)

5 See, for such an account, Morris Kline, *Mathematics: The Loss of Certainty* (Oxford, 1980). Aspects of the argument are controversial and are contested in, for instance, Fernando Zalamea, *Synthetic Philosophy of Contemporary Mathematics* (Falmouth, 2012).

6 Jeremy Gray, *Plato's Ghost: The Modernist Transformation of Mathematics* (Princeton, 2008).

7 Brian Massumi, *Parables for the Virtual: Movement, Affect, Sensation* (Durham, 2002), p. 137.

8 The impact of informational thinking on such fields can be traced in documents such as, Thomas A. Sebeok, *Perspectives in Zoosemiotics* (The Hague, 1972).

9 Stephen Jay Gould, *Wonderful Life: The Burgess Shale and the Nature of History* (London, 2000).

10 Gordon M. Burghardt, *The Genesis of Animal Play: Testing the Limits* (Cambridge, 2005).

11 For a discussion of devastation, see, Matthew Fuller and Olga Goriunova, "Devastation," in *General Ecology: The New Ecological Paradigm,* eds. Erich Hoerl and James Burton (London, 2017), pp. 323–44.

12 Richard J. Hobbs et al., *Novel Ecosystems: Intervening in the New Ecological World Order* (Oxford, 2013).

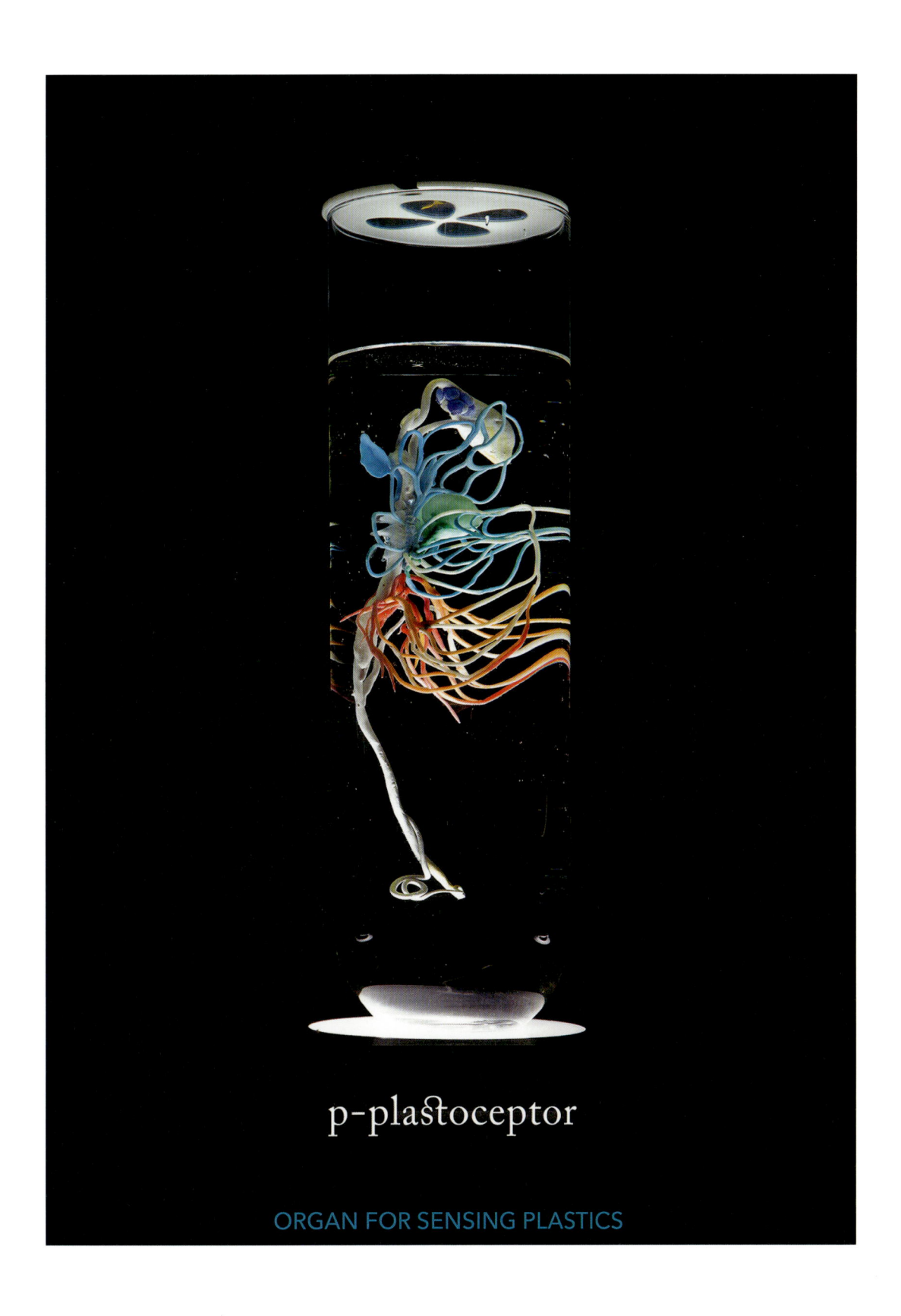

Pinar Yoldas, *P-plastoceptor (organ for sensing plastics)*, from *An Ecosystem of Excess*, 2014

The Center for Genomic Gastronomy, *Post-National Dish: Portugal,* 2017–ongoing

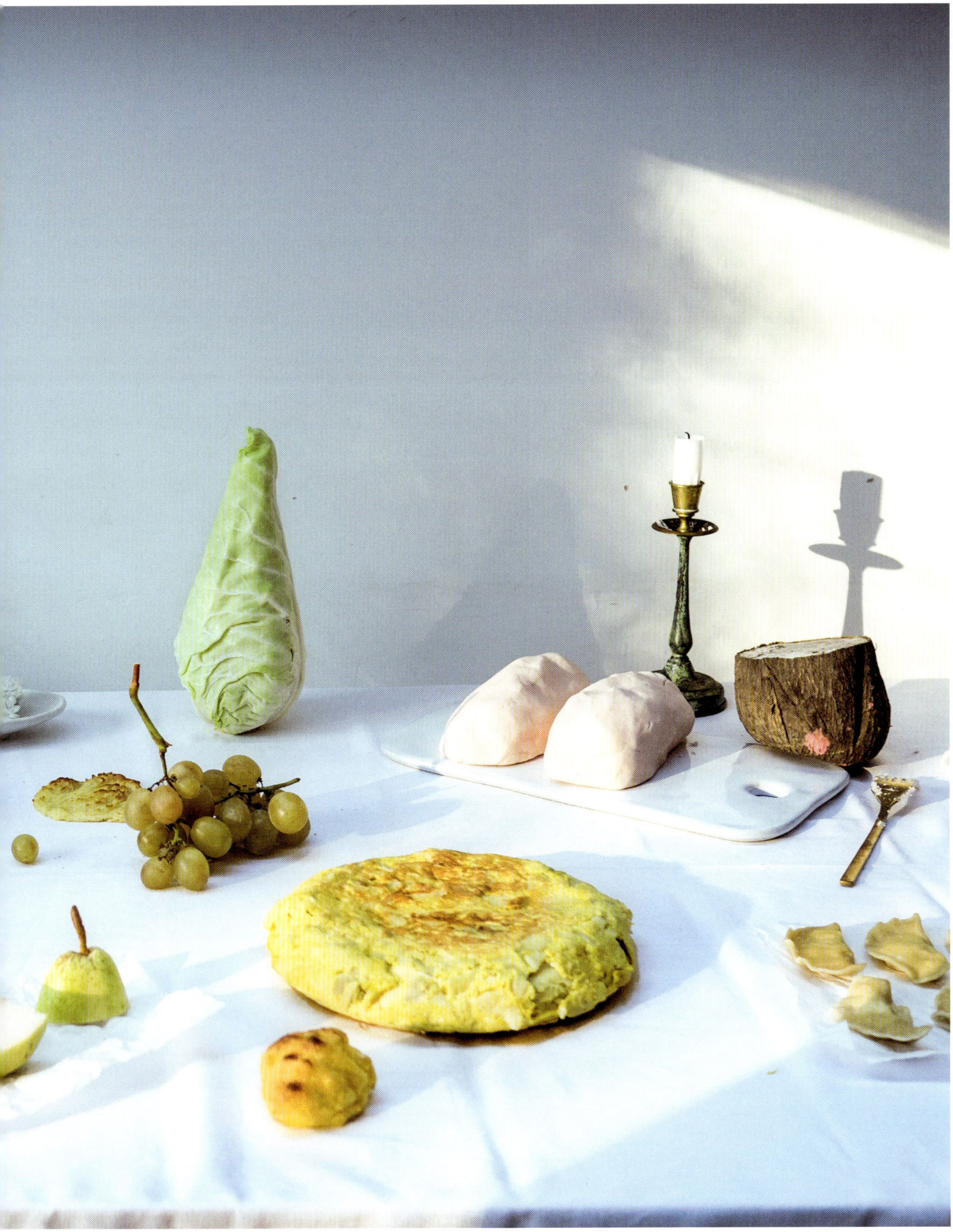

Superflex, *Flooded McDonald's,* 2009, video still

143

Miguel Soares, *Place in Time,* 2005, video stills

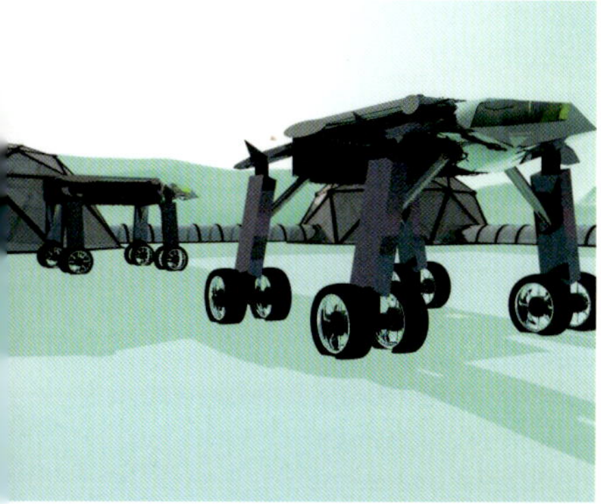

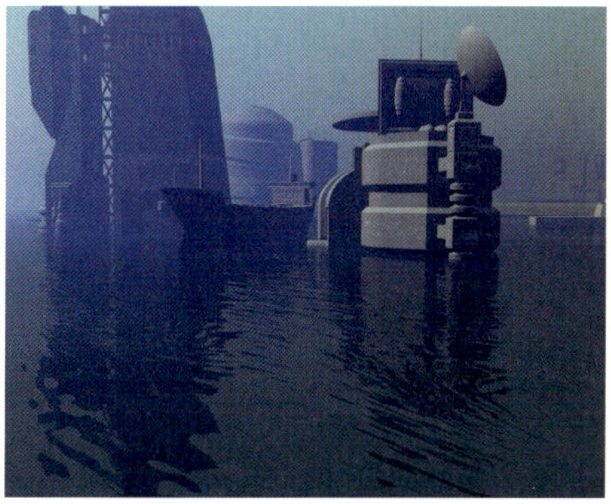

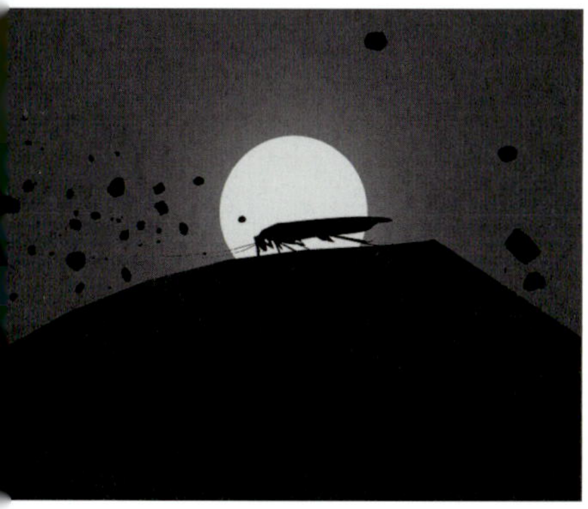

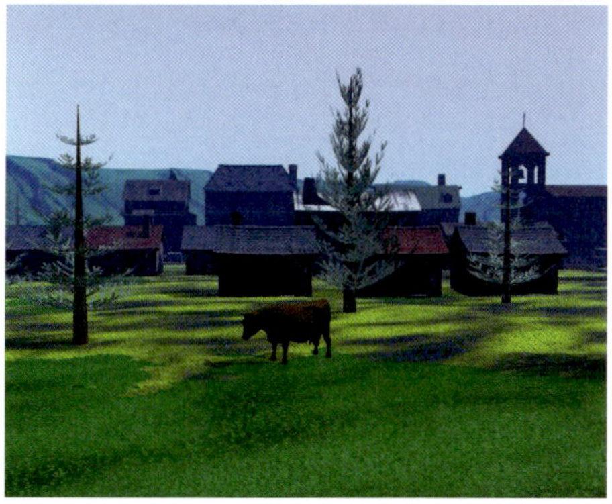

Ursula Biemann, *Acoustic Ocean,* 2018, video stills

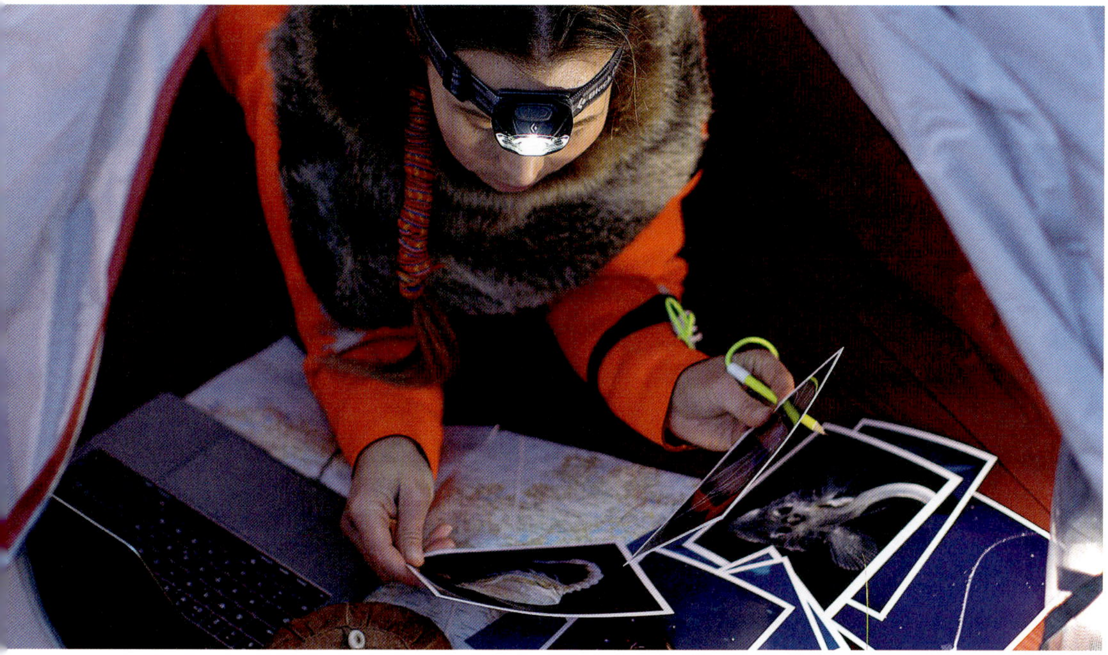

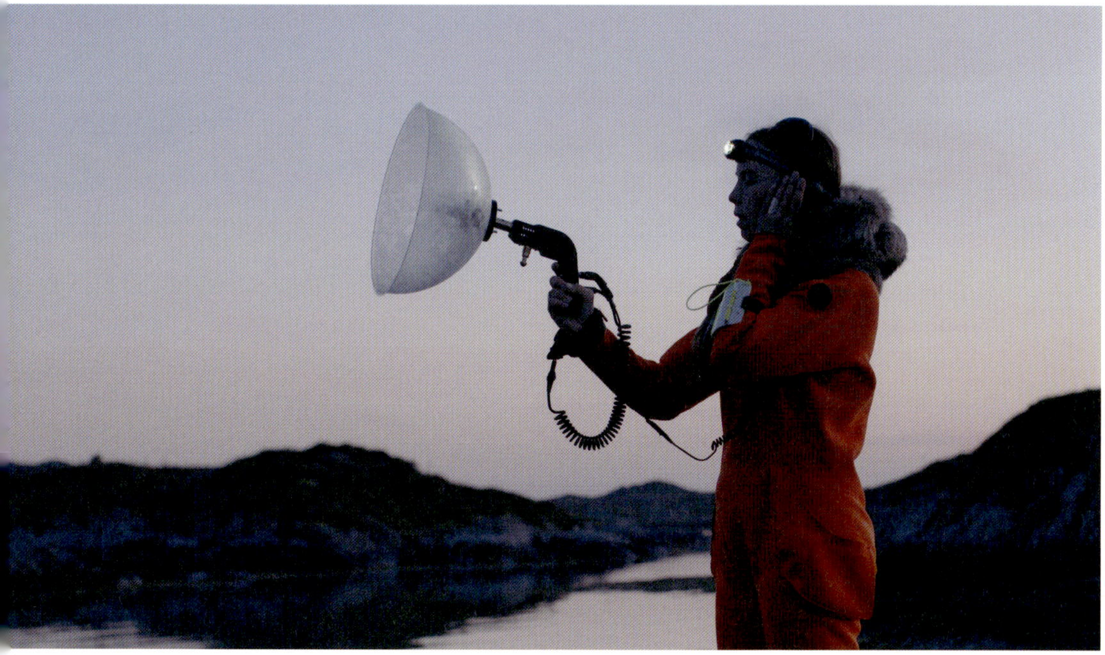

# THE ARTS OF LIVING AT THE END OF THE WORLD

*T. J. DEMOS*

*Our world has come to an end*—part of the phrase's shock is its very familiarity. Visualized repeatedly in an endless stream of pop-cultural dystopian media—movies, games, cable TV—that variously show zombie apocalypses, planetary collisions, and unnatural disasters, the assertion has also now been legitimized scientifically by leading geologists and climatologists, if for different reasons. These have concluded that the world of the Holocene, in existence for the last 12,000 years, has ended, transformed into a crisis of global proportions, a crisis seeking a name. Some call it the Anthropocene, when Earth's natural systems become driven by human activities—in particular humans associated with the institutions of the long historical unfolding of fossil-fuel capitalism, as others who prefer the term Capitalocene importantly point out.[1] In any case, weather events, polar ice melt, forest fires, global warming are all entering catastrophic extremes without historical analogue, signaling even more alarming near-future mortalities—mass species extinctions, the collapse of our environmental support system, even the termination of life's capacities for ongoingness—worsening, if nothing is done to stop runaway climate breakdown.

Zak Ové, *Lost Souls II*, 2011

Rimini Protokoll, *win > < win*, 2017

At this moment, we gaze toward an uninhabitable Earth as one possible future, a world-without-us, a prospect glimpsed as well in the tragic aftermaths of so many recent super-hurricanes, infernos, and disastrous floods.[2] This, at a time when our political systems appear more dysfunctional than ever, headed increasingly toward illiberal governance, authoritarian capitalism, military neoliberalism. Wendy Brown terms it "apocalyptic populism," the willingness of multitudes in thrall to conservative media, racial resentment, and despairing nihilism to entertain the world's destruction—by supporting extremist regimes, exit strategies of self-annihilation, bordered isolationism, and bombing problems away—rather than countenance political movements for socioeconomic equality, anti-racist solidarity, and environmental leadership.[3]

We are at an historic crossing of momentous proportions, and its morbid symptomatology—depressive emotional states, political nihilism, cultural escapism—is being investigated extensively in diverse cultural theory and philosophy, anthropology and media studies.[4] Yet rifts are appearing too, breaks in the ruling order. Consider the proposals of climatologists and environmental social-movement leaders, theorists of the so-called Great Transition, Leap Manifesto, and Climate Mobilization—such as James Hansen and Kevin Anderson, Naomi Klein and Bill McKibben—who have supplied roadmaps for how to get to a world beyond fossil-fuel dependency, one that is, crucially, both ecologically sustainable and socially just. Yet, while much needed, these technology-oriented programs are largely conceptually defined information campaigns, pragmatic and rational, which tend to speak to those already supportive of their visions; as such, they are far from mobilizing the wide-scale public support necessary for successful implementation. In fact, it often feels as if we are moving in an opposite, regressive direction, politically as much as environmentally, toward further embraces of apocalyptic populism.

The key question remains how we can transform our *values* at fundamental levels. How can we collectively move away from functioning as "carbon subjects," thoroughly locked into petrocapitalism's deathly logic of possessive individualism and mindless growth, and instead *become otherwise,* embracing commitments supportive of interspecies justice, environmental mutualism, social wellbeing, communal emancipation, and ecological flourishing?[5] Moreover, how do we inspire the desires to resist self-destruction in the first place, when the only world many know is one of beyond-grotesque economic disparity, racist xenophobia, and lifeless 24/7 labor—or worse, persistent, involuntary unemployment, eased by opiate addiction—under late settler liberalism and its destruction of any worth beyond that measured by commercial metrics and material possession? Indeed, why save a world, many might ask, built upon centuries of colonialism and slavery, a world that is, with its expanding privatized prisons and inescapable systems of debt-servitude, still in their grips? There is little doubt that if environmentalism fails to address *these* fundamental questions, then such environmentalism needs to be rescued from the environmentalists.

This is precisely where cultural and artistic experimentation become urgent, even life-saving, as their ambitious, path-breaking creativity offers an imagination capable of restoring belief in alternative worlds, and generating the energies necessary to realize them. Not only can the arts function as a critical lens exposing situations of injustice—one might consider

*Forest Law,* the video installation of Ursula Biemann and Paulo Tavares that uncovers decades of disastrous oil drilling in the Ecuadorian Amazon, or Angela Melitopoulos's *Crossings,* shown recently at Documenta 14, that depicts conflicts over gold mining and debt servitude in Greece. They also provide speculative and researched accounts of potential alternative futures, collaborative systems of doing things otherwise, such as those glimpsed by rights of nature jurisprudence, the recognition of Indigenous sovereignty, creative practices of mutual aid, and ways of imagining multispecies democracy. What is remarkable about such artistic practices is how they materialize values in their experimental realm of creativity that are radically distinct from conventional systems of belief, where we can perceive and imaginatively inhabit spaces of aesthetic sensation—defining the cultural forms of images and stories that help order our lives—that are dedicated to the concepts and affects of justice, mutualism, cooperation. The arts map other worlds, rescuing us from a future already—but importantly, never fully—colonized by petrocapitalism. More, such aesthetic constructions destabilize and transgress the clear boundaries between art and life, where the perception and inhabitation of new or different modes of being become imaginable and that much more possible, including the recognition that profoundly different forms of life already exist in the here and now.

If politics have long been considered the art of the possible, their conventional forms, it appears, commonly serve to lock us into the pragmatic and familiar, even the bureaucratic and policed (especially wherever it serves corporate interests), beyond which, we are told, there is no alternative. The situation is not so different in institutional spaces of artistic presentation—the commercial galleries, museums, auction houses, and their discursive spaces of dissemination in for-profit journals and magazines. They tend to reinforce codified modes of practice and spectatorship obeying strict limits of political engagement, even while the rhetoric of duty-free aesthetic autonomy (in this case, the autonomy *from* political engagement) is continually proclaimed. Against this mode of capitalist realism, the most ambitious arts—when alternately and experimentally conceived—insist on the necessity of the imaginable.[6] With radical artistic positions we confront the renewed possibility of the political.

That is, as long as the arts themselves are not dominated by the commodity form, serving private interests that are often politically regressive, removing us from the urgencies of addressing life at the end of the world and helping to create what comes next. Among the theoretical resources that can help articulate the terms of this argument are the well-established writings of French philosopher and psychotherapist Félix Guattari, who claimed that any systematic transformation of politics—understood in the broadest sense of how we collectively organize life—requires passing through aesthetics toward "the arts of the living." His provocative account offers a prescient modeling of what I would term an eco-politics of intersectionality today. Politics requires a re-foundation via an "ethico-aesthetic paradigm" that entails an interlinked transformation of subjectivity, sociality, and environment (the basis of Guattari's *The Three Ecologies*). That transformation means that the "greenhouse effect" cannot be solved without also addressing a "mutation of mentality," achieving, for instance, a post-sexist and anti-racist subjectivity. That requires in turn overcoming "Third World" debt-servitude and impoverishment and a critique of conventional "modes of valorization," challenging the privileging of economic growth above all else, according to the repressive terms of "Integrated World Capitalism."[7] In other words, meaningfully addressing the climate

Ursula Biemann and Paulo Tavares, *Forest Law*, 2014

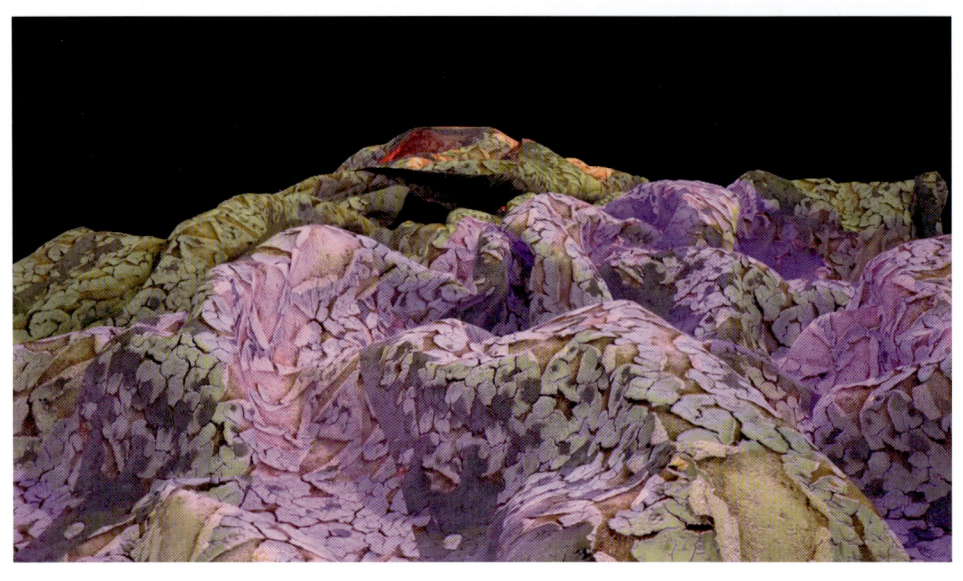

Eva Papamargariti, *Precarious Inhabitants*, 2017, video stills

challenge is not simply a matter of talking about atmospheric carbon, but must extend into diverse and interlinked socio-subjective relations and environmental geopolitics, all of which contribute to how we conceptualize, define, and actualize the world(s) we live in.

There are many aspects of Guattari's prescient account that continue to resonate in significance, only appearing to have grown in relevance from today's perspective, three in particular I will elaborate. First, with this conceptualization of "the arts of the living" we encounter the radical expansion of creative practice beyond commercial and institutional enclosure, beyond art's objectification and relegation to consumerism, decoration, and markets of material growth, coming on the heels of conceptualism's dematerialization of the object that has equally been transformed into a capitalist experience economy. The arts of the living entail the transformation of the way we organize social and material reproduction, which unleashes creativity from institutional containment and sees it flourishing in creative ecologies of practice—from growing food biodynamically to organizing biopolitical assemblages as a form of blockading petrocapitalist infrastructural development, from anti-racist organizations of mutual aid living outside the capitalist wage economy to knowledge-sharing beyond the codified markets for academic and industry publications. Such intersectionalist positions resonate with the diverse, interdisciplinary, and social-practice-based work of such practitioners as Amy Balkin and her investigation of law and environmentalism, Maria Thereza Alves's inquiry into the colonial-era diaspora of seeds, the Futurefarmers' examination of biodiversity and food systems (pp. 104–05), and Superflex's contributions to democratized energy sources (pp. 140–41). Of course there are many more relevant practices. Guattari's view certainly reaffirms avant-garde strategies like Joseph Beuys's model of "social sculpture" and the like, but resists its subsequent capture within the immaterial labor models of practice that have transformed into the depoliticized sites of relational aesthetics—in this sense it corresponds as well with proposals to decolonize aesthetics, rescuing them from Euro-American institutional hegemony.[8] Rather, the arts of the living offer a conceptualization of what philosophers including Jacques Rancière and Judith Butler might call "the redistribution of the sensible" that extends aesthetics with political definition into everyday life, where aesthetics take on a generative power to reinvent the conditions of life in ways positively linked to social justice, emancipatory ambition, and ecological wellbeing.

Second, with the arts of the living, aesthetics are joined to ethics, not in a way that diverts us from politics by privileging individual private morality, but instead as a commitment to structural and transversal transformations that operate within a newly constructed realm of appearance made equitable. Even if this move remains aspirational, the goal is an inclusive visual and auditory field operating in relation to Guattari's triplet of subjective experience, social relationality, and ecological connectivity. The ambition is nothing less than broadening the scope of ecology (the science of connectivity between organisms and their environments) as a format of *intersectionality*—the practice defined initially within African-American juridical-feminist analysis of the interjoined conditions of gendered and racialized forms of oppression, which equally proposes the necessarily interconnected terms of emancipation.[9] In other words, it is not accurate or politically enabling to say that climate change situates us humans in "a war against nature," armed with atmospheric carbon, threatening to subject all to mass heat death—as Bill McKibben, founder of 350.org, has argued.[10] The problem is not only that such a view diverts us from recognizing the *causes* of climate breakdown in petrocapitalism; it also fails to comprehend the differential *impacts* of environmental transformation that affect the impoverished and disenfranchised more than others (case in point was the catastrophic 2017 hurricane season and the damage wreaked in Puerto Rico, damage that cannot be divorced from, and in fact exacerbates, the political and economic violence implemented through decades of neocolonial US financial policy[11]). Consider in this light Natalie Jeremijenko's art of biochemistry and transformative social change; Marjetica Potrč's social architectures of emancipation (pp. 101–03); and Design Earth's investigations into the flows, ecologies, and logistics of waste (p. 77), all of which interlink natures and cultures, economics and environments, politics and aesthetics.

Third, the arts of the living challenge modes of *valorization,* including how we understand the very being and relationality of objects. In this sense, the work of Guattari, including that emerging from his important collaboration with Gilles Deleuze, defines an important philosophical precursor that has prepared the ground for more recent theoretical advances, including the ontological turn and new materialisms, the politics of multinaturalism and its challenging of the mononaturalist limits of multiculturalism, and the various subjective and social becomings that transcend anthropocentrism and human exceptionalism.[12] Indeed, the arts, for Deleuze and Guattari, materialize an affective intensification of percepts and concepts, including those of politics and science, which offer functional matrixes, ever evolving, that organize and revise our cultural frames of reference.[13] In other words, rethinking the way we value objects—expanding to human attributes, nonhuman beings, nature, hyperobjects of relational assemblages such as ecosystems undergoing climate change—points to nothing less than an emergent politics of "geontology," concerning the being of the world. According to anthropologist Elizabeth Povinelli, geontopolitics defines a set of discourses, affects, and tactics used to maintain and shape the distinction between life and nonlife, determining, for instance, whether we see water fundamentally as an exploitable commodity within the system of petrocapitalism, or as a living and integral element of our complex life world. Such a conflict recently came to a head at Standing Rock, and, more broadly, offers another way to name the very crisis that is at stake between radically different worlds today[14]— such is visualized and charted, for instance, in the work of Biemann and Tavares, Lara Almárcegui's art of urban material transformations, Tue Greenfort's examinations of eco-economics (p. 161), and Henrik Håkansson's inquiries into post-natures and entangled techno-ecologies.

How do we best survive the Anthropocene's destructive human-centric sovereignty, the Capitalocene's financialization of everything according to a generalized logic of extraction, fostering extreme economic inequality? How can we embrace an ethics of multispecies being and institute legal protocols for its recognition and enforcement? What are our current cultural resources capable of supporting a Great Transition, not only of our energy systems, but also of our fundamental values, embracing hope for a passage beyond petrocapitalism's coming end and toward a world of equality founded on ecology? And in defining such resources, how have the arts themselves undergone profound shifts—moving away from aestheticist culturalism, institutionalized commercial objects, and representations of unrealizable utopias, and toward new models of creative and activist world-making practices, marking rifts in the present system as well as opening up passages of life beyond the end of the world? What

MVRDV, *Pig City*, 2000

possible futures do the artworks of eco-visionaries announce, what kinds of *re-worldings,* in the language of Donna Haraway, do they make visible?[15] These are the key questions we all need to consider.

By exploring the cultural recognition of the end of the world as registered in some of the most far-reaching artistic expressions of our day, we can read our present juncture as not simply historical, but sociopolitical and philosophical, as well as *aesthetic,* in the most fundamental of ways: as a matter of seeing and hearing. To live beyond the end of the Holocene requires a discerning perception, invoking nothing less than a paradigm shift of sensibility, even in the face of its increased disciplinary regulation and policed visuality, at a time when what is imaged—pipelines, border crossings, extraction sites—is strictly regulated, surveilled, even criminalized. Nonetheless, new worlds are emerging beyond our outmoded one that is so violently unequal, militarized and racialized, unsustainable and necropolitical. Creative practitioners from diverse artistic and cultural engagements have provided glimpses of potential futures beyond our current impasse. Doing so, they have begun to investigate what such a transition—in its most ambitious of senses—would look like and mean, how it might be lived and expressed.

---

1   See Jason W. Moore, ed., *Anthropocene or Capitalocene: Nature, History, and the Crisis of Capitalism* (Oakland, 2016); T. J. Demos, A*gainst the Anthropocene: Visual Culture and Environment Today* (Berlin, 2017).

2   David Wallace-Wells, "The Uninhabitable Earth," *New York Magazine,* July 9, 2017, http://nymag.com/daily/intelligencer/2017/07/climate-change-earth-too-hot-for-humans.html (accessed October, 2017).

3   Wendy Brown, "Apocalyptic Populism," *Eurozine,* August 30, 2017, http://www.eurozine.com/apocalyptic-populism/ (accessed October, 2017). Here she points to the phenomena of Trump, Brexit, and the European crisis of democracy in the face of migration as central examples (accessed October, 2017).

4   I am thinking of Timothy Morton's *Hyperobjects: Philosophy and Ecology After the End of the World* (Minneapolis, 2013); Eduardo Viveiros de Castro and Déborah Danowski, *The Ends of the World* (New York, 2017); Elizabeth Povinelli, *Geontologies: A Requiem to Late Liberalism* (Durham, 2016).

5   Andreas Malm, *Fossil Capital: The Rise of Steam Power and the Roots of Global Warming* (London, 2016).

6   Mark Fisher, *Capitalist Realism: Is there no Alternative?* (London, 2009).

7   Felix Guattari, *Chaosmosis: An Ethico-Aesthetic Paradigm,* trans. Paul Bains and Julian Pefanis (Bloomingdale, 1995), p. 21; Félix Guattari, *The Three Ecologies,* trans. Ian Pindar and Paul Sutton (London, 2000), p. 69.

8   See Walter Mignolo and Rolando Vazquez, "Decolonial AestheSis: Colonial Wounds/Decolonial Healings," *Social Text Online,* July 15, 2013, http://socialtextjournal.org/periscope_article/decolonial-aesthesis-colonial-woundsdecolonial-healings/ (accessed October, 2017).

9   Kimberle Crenshaw, "Mapping the Margins: Intersectionality, Identity Politics, and Violence against Women of Color," *Stanford Law Review* 43, no. 6 (July 1991), pp. 1241–99; T. J. Demos, "Ecology-as-Intersectionality," *The Distance Plan Journal* 4 (2016), p. 25.

10  Bill McKibben, "A World at War: We're Under Attack from Climate Change—and Our Only Hope Is to Mobilize Like We Did in WWII," *New Republic,* August 15, 2016, https://newrepublic.com/article/135684/declare-war-climate-change-mobilize-wwii (accessed October, 2017).

11  See Nelson Denis, "After a Century of American Citizenship, Puerto Ricans Have Little to Show for It," *The Nation,* March 2, 2017, https://www.thenation.com/article/after-a-century-of-american-citizenship-puerto-ricans-have-little-to-show-for-it/ (accessed October, 2017); Vijay Prashad, "A Tale of Two Islands," *Frontline,* October 23, 2017, http://www.frontline.in/world-affairs/a-tale-of-two-islands/article9892265.ece (accessed October, 2017).

12  Povinelli, 2016 (see note 4), p. 53. Indeed, she writes, central to the recent work of speculative realism and new materialism "is a deep and creative engagement with Gilles Deleuze's idea of the assemblage and event. This gravitation to Deleuze and his longtime partner, Félix Guattari, is hardly surprising. Not only does their approach demand that we see the potential for actualization, deactualization, and reactualization in any arrangement of existence, they do so through a language that draws on geological, ecological, and geometrical metaphors more than biological ones, and thus appear to provide critical theory an exit from the prisonhouse of biontology."

13  See Gilles Deleuze and Félix Guattari, *What is Philosophy?*, trans. Hugh Tomlinson and Graham Burchell III (New York, 1996), p. 164.

14  Povinelli, 2016 (see note 4), p. 4.

15  Donna Haraway, *Staying with the Trouble: Making Kin in the Chthulucene* (Durham, 2016).

Nelly Ben Hayoun, *Disaster Playground,* 2015

Tue Greenfort, *Tilapia #09*, 2017

Juanjo Palacios, *Reserva Sonora de la Biosfera de Asturias: Mapa sonoro v 1.0*, 2018

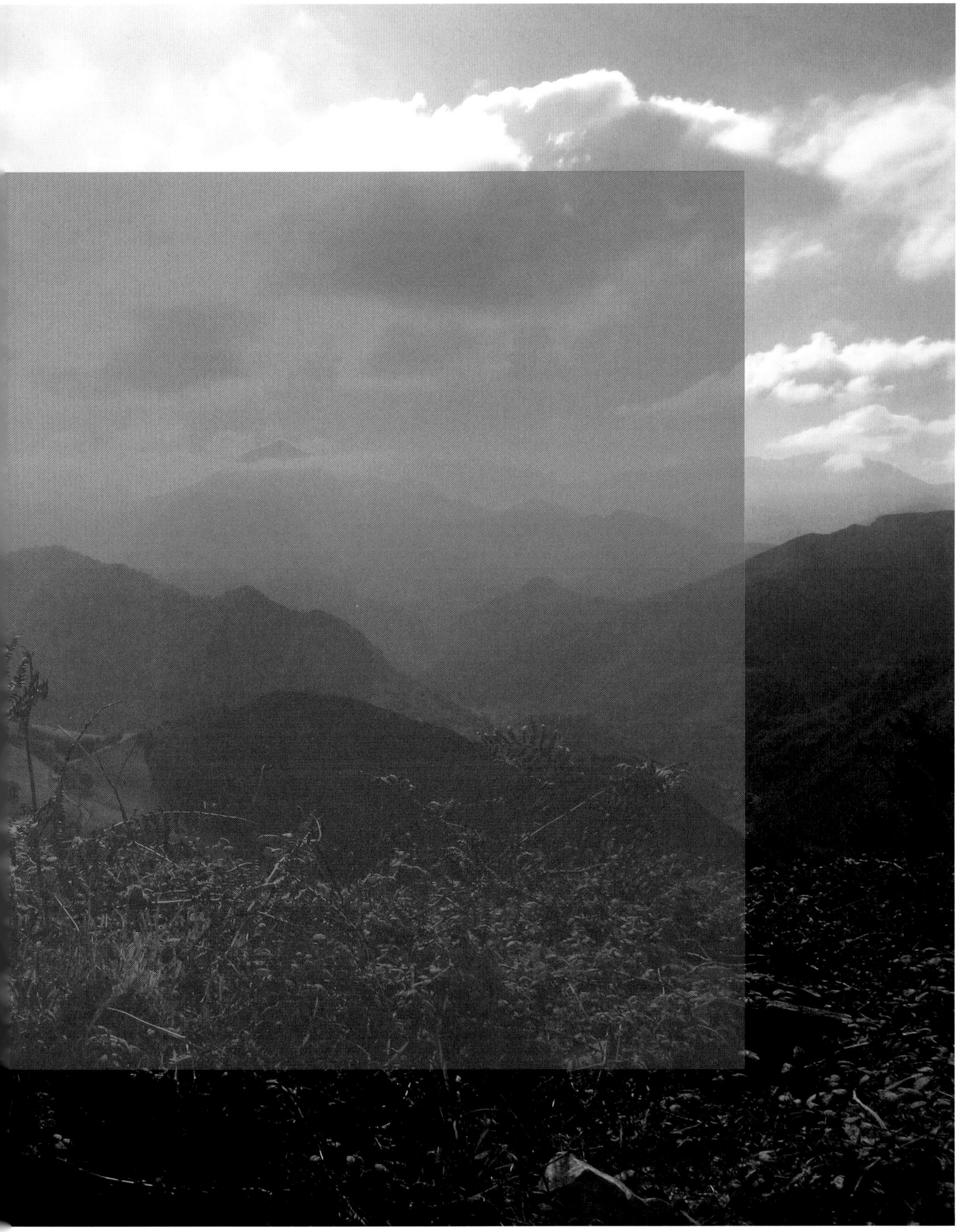

Daniel Arsham, *Future Relic 04*, 2015, production photo

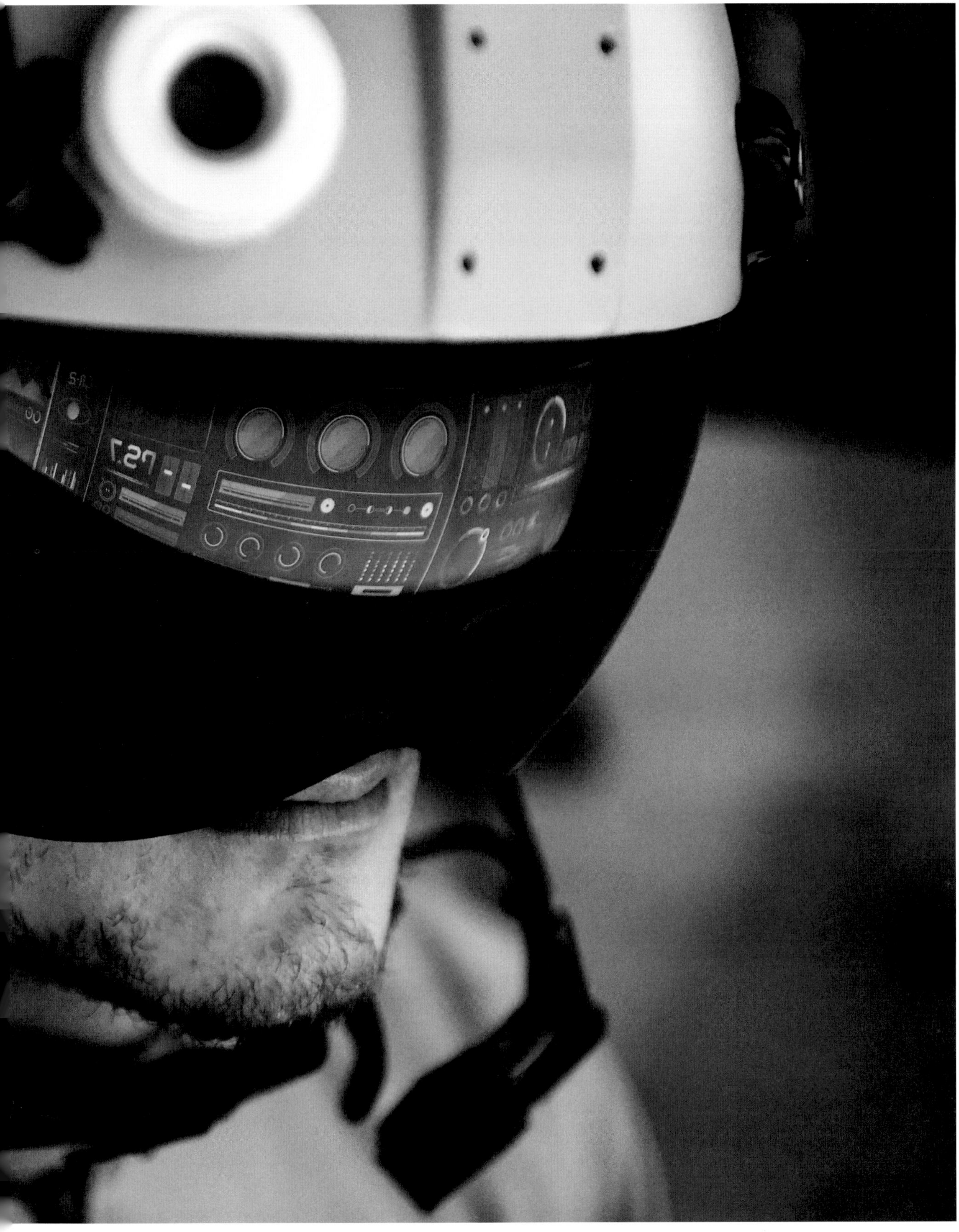

HeHe, *Domestic Catastrophe N° 3: La Planète Laboratoire*, 2012

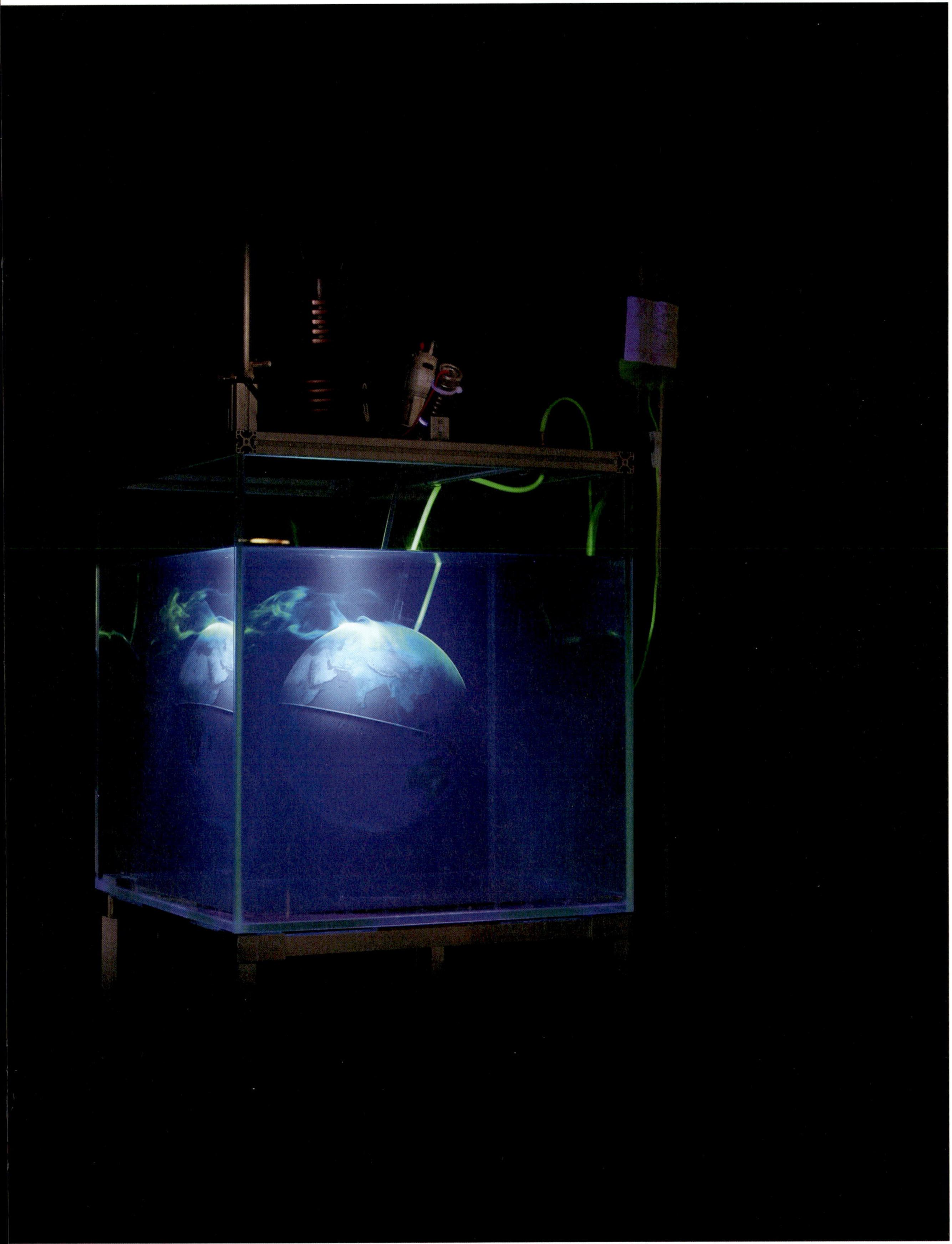

Tomás Saraceno, *A Thermodynamic Imaginary,* 2018, view of the exhibition at MAAT, 2018

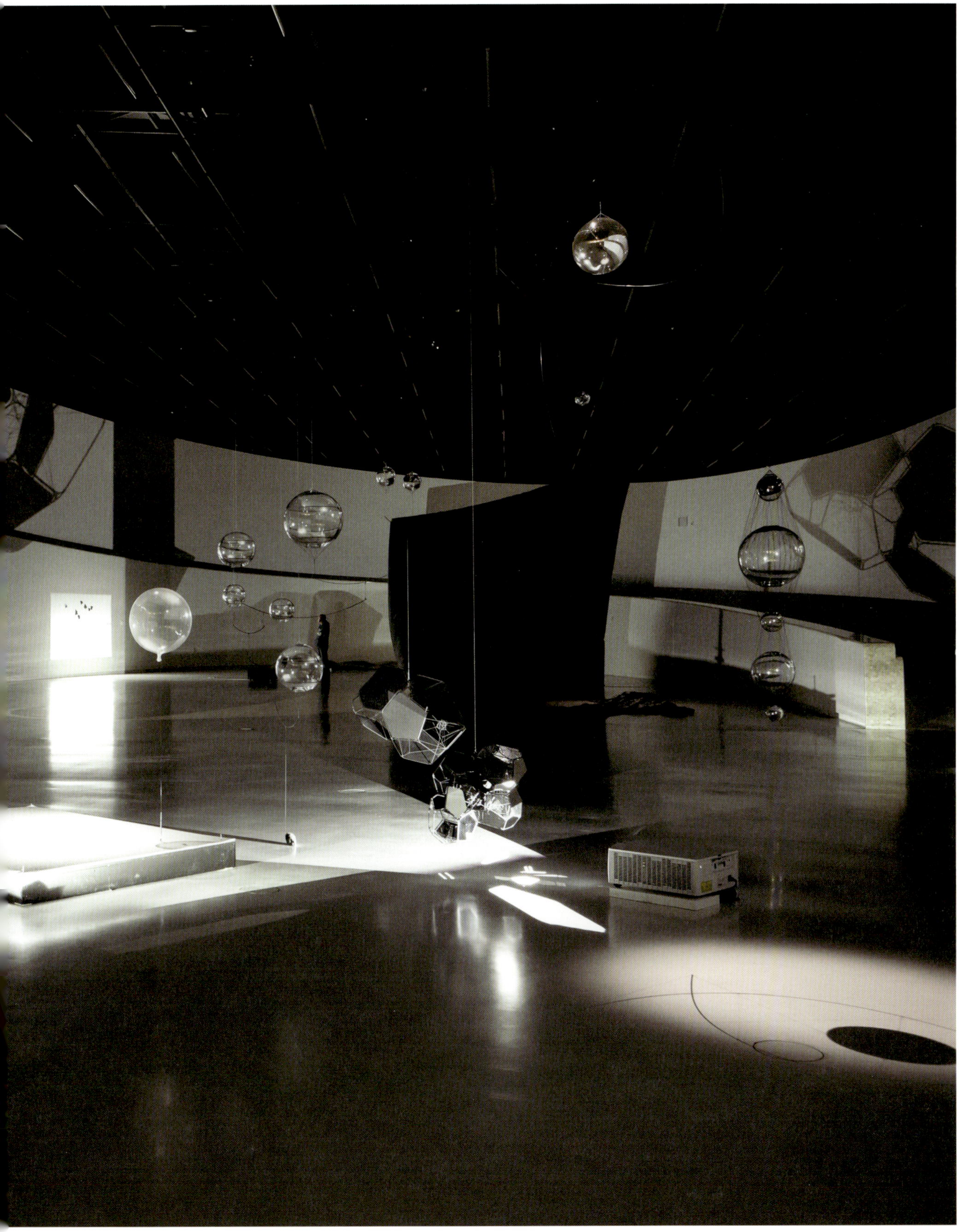

# LIST OF WORKS

Robert Smithson,
*Partially Buried Woodshed,* 1970

© Heirs of Robert Smithson, VAGA, New York / SPA, Lisbon, 2018
(p. 37)

WORKac and Ant Farm,
*3.C.City: Climate, Convention, Cruise,* 2015

Courtesy of the authors
(p. 58)

SITE, *Forest Building,*
Best Products Company,
Richmond, VA, 1980

Courtesy of James Newton Wines
(p. 60)

Elin Már Øyen Vister at work

Photo by Jason Rosenberg
(p. 94)

José Gualingua, leader of the Kichwa people of Sarayaku, Ecuador, from *Forest Law* by Ursula Biemann and Paulo Tavares

Courtesy of the authors
(p. 97)

Collective action during the 32nd Bienal de São Paulo, 2016. Published on Carolina Caycedo's Instagram account (@lacaycedo), November 5, 2016

Courtesy of the author
(p. 97)

Photo of Lars-Evert Nutti inspecting arboreal lichen, Boden, 2009

Courtesy of Samuel Roturier
(p. 95)

## LIST OF WORKS ORGANISED BY EXHIBITIONS

### MAAT

Tomás Saraceno with the Aerocene Foundation
*A Thermodynamic Imaginary*

Installation at MAAT (Oval Gallery, March 21–August 27, 2018)
Courtesy of the artist; Aerocene Foundation; Andersen's Contemporary, Copenhagen; Ruth Benzakar, Buenos Aires; Tanya Bonakdar Gallery, New York; Pinksummer Contemporary Art, Genoa; Esther Schipper, Berlin
Photo by Bruno Lopes, courtesy of EDP Foundation
(pp. 168–69)

The Harrison Studio
(founded in the USA, 1970)
*The Second Lagoon—Sea Grant, The Lagoon Cycle,* 1973–84

Reproduction
Courtesy of Newton and Helen Mayer Harrison
(p. 38)

Haus-Rucker-Co
(founded in Austria, 1967–92)
*Environment Transformer,* 1968

Reproduction
© Haus-Rucker-Co, Gerald Zugmann
(p. 35)

Skrei (founded in Portugal, 2009)
*Biogas Power Plant,* 2017

Iron, earthwork, marine plywood, domestic organic waste;
200 × 150 × 150 cm
Courtesy of the authors
(p. 51)

Wasted Rita (Portugal, 1988)
*The Future Is Written,* 2016

Mixed media installation;
dimensions variable
Courtesy of the author and Underdogs Gallery, Lisbon.
Views of the installation at Festival Iminente, Oeiras, 2016
(pp. 44–45)

Krištof Kintera (Czech Republic, 1973)
*Postnaturalia Herbario Plate,* 2016

Mixed media; 103 × 73 cm (each)
Courtesy of the author
(p. 43)

Parsons & Charlesworth
(Tim Parsons, 1974, UK, and Jessica Charlesworth, 1979, UK)
*The BioPhotovoltaics Hacktivist,*
from *New Survivalism,* 2014

Mixed media, 55 × 55 × 40 cm (closed)
Courtesy of the authors
Photos by Jonathan Allen
(pp. 48–49)

Ana Vaz and Tristan Bera
(Brazil, 1986, and France, 1984)
*A Film, Reclaimed,* 2015

Video, HD, 16:9, color, 5.1 surround sound;
19 min. 36 sec.
Courtesy of the authors
(pp. 90–91)

Wanuri Kahiu (Kenya, 1980)
*Pumzi,* 2009

Video, HD, 1920 × 1080, color, sound; 23 min. 52 sec.
Courtesy of the author
(pp. 30–31)

Basim Magdy (Egypt, 1977)
*Our Prehistoric Fate,* 2011

Duraclear prints, metal light box displays, metal clamps; 2 prints, 138 × 162 cm
Edition of 3 + 1 AP
Courtesy of the author and Gypsum Gallery
(pp. 26–27)

Superuse
(founded in the Netherlands, 1997)
*Harvestmap Platform: Blue City,*
2012–ongoing

Installation; dimensions variable
Courtesy of the authors
(p. 63)

Ant Farm (founded in USA, 1968–78)
*Clean Air Pod* at the Air Emergency event, 1970

Performance, lower Sproul Plaza, University of California, Berkeley
Reproduction
University of California, Berkeley Art Museum and Pacific Film Archive
© Chip Lord
(p. 57)

Buckminster Fuller (USA, 1895–1983) and Shoji Sadao (USA, 1927)
*Dome Over Manhattan*, 1960

Reproduction
Courtesy of the Estate of R. Buckminster Fuller
(p. 59)

Andrés Jaque (1971, Spain) with Patrick Craine / Office for Political Innovation (founded in Spain, 2003)
*Island House in Laguna Grande, Corpus Christi, Texas*, 2015–ongoing

Architecture project
Courtesy of the authors
(pp. 32–33)

Design Crew for Architecture (founded in France, 2007)
*Freshwater Factory Skyscraper*, 2010

Architecture project
Courtesy of the authors
(pp. 64–65)

Malka Architecture (founded in France, 2003)
*The Green Machine*, 2014

Architecture project
Courtesy of the authors
(p. 53)

MVRDV (founded in The Netherlands, 1991)
*Pig City*, 2000

Architecture project
Courtesy of the authors
(p. 157)

BIG (founded in Denmark, 2005)
*Amager Resource Center*, 2013

Architecture project
Courtesy of the authors
(pp. 68–69)

The Living (founded in USA, 2006)
*Hy-Fi*, 2014

Video, sound; 2 min. 43 sec.
Courtesy of the authors
(p. 61)

John Gerrard (Ireland, 1947)
*Western Flag (Spindletop, Texas)*, 2017

Simulation; dimensions variable
Courtesy of the authors
Commissioned by Channel 4 for broadcast on Earth Day, April 22, 2017, and presented in partnership with Somerset House
(p. 73)

HeHe (founded in France, 1999)
*Catastrophes Domestiques N°2: Prise en Charge*, 2011

Electric socket, fog machine, timer; dimensions variable
Courtesy of the authors and Aeroplastics, Brussels
(pp. 70–71)

Ornaghi & Prestinari (Valentina Ornaghi, Italy, 1986, and Claudio Prestinari, Italy, 1984)
*Asmatico*, 2015–16

Aluminum cast, stainless steel, bulb, hazer machine; 85 × 120 × 80 cm
Courtesy of the authors and Galleria Continua, San Gimignano, Beijing, Les Moulins, Habana
(p. 74)

Design Earth (Rania Ghosn, Lebanon, 1977, and El Hadi Jazairy, Algeria, 1970)
*Trash Peaks*, 2017

Printed silk on wood, 3D-printed ceramics, printed carpet; dimensions variable
Courtesy of the artists
Photos by Kyungsub Shin
(p. 77)

Territorial Agency (John Palmesino, Switzerland, 1970, and Ann-Sofi Rönnskog, Finland, 1976)
*Museum of Oil*, 2016

Digital print on alu-dibond mounted on a metal frame; 600 × 305 cm
Courtesy of the artists
Photos by Harald Völkl, view of the installation at ZKM, Karlsruhe
(p. 78)

Kiluanji Kia Henda (Angola, 1979)
*Havemos de Voltar (We Shall Return)*, 2017

Video, single-channel, color, sound; 17 min. 30 sec.
Courtesy of the author
(pp. 88–89)

Rimini Protokoll (founded in Germany, 2000)
*win > < win*, 2017

Installation; dimensions variable
A Rimini Protokoll production (Helgard Kim Haug, Stefan Kaegi, Daniel Wetzel), technical project by Alejandro Olariaga, audio project and synchronization by Carlos Gómez, with the participation of Jamileh Javidpour, Daniel Strozynski, Lisa-Ann Gershwin, Boris Koch, Josep Maria Gili
Commissioned for the exhibition *After the End of the World*, curated by José Luis de Vicente, produced by Centre de Cultura Contemporània de Barcelona with FACT+BLUECOAT+ RIBA NORTH, Liverpool
Photos by Martí E. Berenguer
(p. 150)

Jeremy Shaw (Canada, 1977)
*Liminals*, 2017

Video installation, HD; 31 min. 25 sec.
Courtesy of the author and König Galerie, Berlin, London
(p. 82)

**Alexandra Daisy Ginsberg** (UK, 1982)
*Designing for the Sixth Extinction*,
2013–15

C-type prints, duratrans and lightbox,
3D-printed models; dimensions variable
Courtesy of the author
Commissioned in 2013 for
*Grow Your Own ... Life After Nature*
at Science Gallery, Dublin
Collection of Ginkgo Bioworks, Boston,
and ZKM, Karlsruhe
(pp. 86–87)

**Dunne & Raby**
(Anthony Dunne, UK, 1964, and
Fiona Raby, Singapore, 1963)
*Designs for an Overpopulated Planet:
Foragers*, 2009

Glass fiber sculptures;
55 × 50 × 35 cm, 160 × 98 × 25 cm
Lambda prints mounted on aluminum;
200 × 150 cm
3D animation, color, sound; 2 min. 53 sec.
Courtesy of the authors
Photos by Jason Evans
(p. 85)

**Philippe Rahm** (Switzerland, 1967)
*Meteorological Architecture*, 2009–11

Video, 31 min. 20 sec.
Courtesy of Philippe Rahm architectes
(p. 67)

**Ursula Biemann** and **Paulo Tavares**
(Switzerland, 1955, and Brazil, 1980)
*Forest Law*, 2014

Two-channel synchronized video projection,
color, sound; 38 min; book, map, text;
dimensions variable
Courtesy of the artist
(p. 153)

**Superflex** (founded in Denmark, 1993)
*Flooded McDonald's*, 2009

Video, 1920 × 1080, color, stereo; 21 min.
Courtesy of the artists
(pp. 140–41)

**Tue Greenfort** (Denmark, 1973)
*Tilapia #02*, 2017

Ink on paper; 70 × 50 cm
Courtesy the artist and Konig Galerie,
Berlin, London
Photo by Roman Marz

**Tue Greenfort** (Denmark, 1973)
*Tilapia #09*, 2017

Ink on paper; 70 × 50 cm
Courtesy the artist and König Galerie,
Berlin, London
Photo by Roman März
(p. 161)

**Pedro Neves Marques**
(Portugal, 1984)
*The Pudic Relation Between
Machine and Plant*, 2016

Video loop, sound; 2 min. 30 sec.
With the support of the Centre for Robotics
Research at King's College, London
Courtesy of the artist
(p. 132)

**Unknown Fields Division**
(founded in UK, 2008)
*The Breast Milk of the Volcano*,
2016–18

Glass, lithium brine, graphite, aluminum;
17.5 × 17.5 × 55 cm;
video, sound, color; 10 min.
Fabricated with assistance from
Eduardo Andreu Gonzalez and Aimer Ltd.,
battery science consultant:
Donal Finegan, film developed in
collaboration with Luca Films
Courtesy of the artists
(p. 81)

**Nelly Ben Hayoun** (France, 1985)
*Disaster Playground*, 2015

Video, sound, color; 65 min.
Emergency jacket, red curtain,
wall logo, podium, and flags;
dimensions variable
Courtesy of the artist
(p. 159)

**Zak Ové** (UK, 1966)
*Lost Souls II*, 2011

Horse skull, skateboard, noise
cancelling headphones, toy airplane,
toy cars, beads, socks, brass frog,
pilot's oxygen mask, cake mold,
mixed media; 150 × 43 × 46 cm
Courtesy of the artist and Vigo Gallery,
London
(p. 149)

**Carolina Caycedo** (England, 1978)
*Serpent River Book*, 2017

Artist book, 72-page accordion fold, offset
print, printed canvas hardcover, elastic band;
22 × 31 × 3.5 cm (closed)
Numbered edition of 250
Courtesy of the author
(p. 99)

**Diller Scofidio + Renfro**
(founded in USA, 1981) with **Mark
Hansen, Laura Kurgan,** and **Ben Rubin,**
in collaboration with **Robert Gerard
Pietrusko** and **Stewart Smith**
*Exit*, 2008–15

Video, single-channel version, stereo sound;
22 min. 44 sec.
Collection of Fondation Cartier pour
l'art contemporain, Paris
© Diller Scofidio + Renfro, Mark Hansen,
Laura Kurgan, Ben Rubin, Stewart Smith,
Robert Gerard Pietrusko
(pp. 46–47)

**Femke Herregraven**
(Netherlands, 1982)
*Sprawling Swamps*, 2016
(ongoing project)

Dynamic interactive virtual environment,
software, sound; dimensions variable
Edition of 3 + 2 AP
Courtesy of the artist and Future Gallery,
Berlin
Photos by Andrea Rossetti
(p. 135)

**Miguel Soares** (Portugal, 1970)
*Place in Time*, 2005

3D animation, DVD, color, sound;
11 min. 30 sec.
Courtesy of the artist
(pp. 144–45)

Daniel Arsham (USA, 1980)
*Future Relic 04,* 2015

Video, color, sound; 9 min. 54 sec.
A film by Daniel Arsham, shot and edited by Ben Nicholas, starring Arturo Castro, Matthew Maher, Ethan Suplee
Courtesy of the artist
Production photos by James Law
(pp. 164–65)

Eva Papamargariti (Greece, 1987)
*Precarious Inhabitants,* 2017

Video, single-channel, 1920 × 1080, color, sound; 13 min. 12 sec.
Edition of 3 + 2 AP
Courtesy of the artist
(p. 154)

The Center for Genomic Gastronomy (founded in USA, 2010)
*Post-National Dish: Portugal,* 2017–ongoing

Environmental research and recipe development
Courtesy of the artists
(pp. 140–41)

Regina Frank—The HeArt is Present (1965, Germany)
*ILand (in sickness in health),* 2018

Tapestry, Egyptian cotton; 404 × 330 cm
Courtesy of the artist
(p. 131)

Pinar Yoldas (Turkey, 1979)
*P-plastoceptor (organ for sensing plastics),* from *An Ecosystem of Excess,* 2014

Resin, tubes, water pump, LED on PVC vase
Courtesy of the artist and White Circle
(p. 139)

**Bildmuseet**

Elin Már Øyen Vister (Norway, 1976)
*Sirkelens ontologi forteller,* 2016–18

Polyphonic composition, sound installation
Courtesy of the author

Samuel Roturier (France, 1982)
*Working with Nature—Sami Reindeer Herders and Biodiversity in the Boreal Forest,* 2016

Video; 14 min.
Courtesy of the author, Lars-Evert Nutti, Jakob Nygård, and Mats-Peter Åstot

Ursula Biemann and Paulo Tavares (Switzerland, 1955, and Brazil, 1980)
*Forest Law,* 2014

Two-channel synchronized video projection, color, sound; 38 min; book, map, text; dimensions variable
Courtesy of the authors
(p. 153)

Leena and Oula A. Valkeapää (Finland, 1964 and 1970)
*Manifestations,* 2017

Video; 15 min.
Courtesy of the authors
(p. 93)

Erik Sjödin (Sweden, 1979)
*The Political Beekeeper's Library,* 2015

Installation, selection of books, bookshelves; dimensions variable
Courtesy of the artist
View of the installation at Art Lab Gnesta, 2015, photo by Erik Sjödin
(p. 96)

Marjetica Potrč (Slovenia, 1953)
*Florestania,* 2006–10

Ink on paper; series of 12 drawings, 21.5 × 27.9 cm (each)
Courtesy of the author and Galerie Nordenhake, Berlin, Stockholm
(p. 101)

Marjetica Potrč (Slovenia, 1953)
*Xapuri: Rural School,* 2006

Building materials, energy and communication infrastructure; dimensions variable
Courtesy of the author and Galerie Nordenhake, Berlin, Stockholm
Installation view by Wolfgang Traeger
Source image courtesy of Seplands and Prodeem, the State of Acre, Brazil
(pp. 102–03)

Carolina Caycedo (England, 1978)
*Land of Friends,* 2014

Single-channel HD video, sound, color; 38 min.
Courtesy of the author
(p. 98)

Carolina Caycedo (England, 1978)
*River Books,* 2016–18

Marker and ink on Canson paper; 4 drawings, 50 × 150 cm (each, approx.)
Courtesy of the author, Commonwealth and Council, Los Angeles, and Instituto de Visión, Bogotá
(p. 98)

Carolina Caycedo (England, 1978)
*Serpent River Book,* 2017

Artist book, 72-page accordion fold, offset print, printed canvas hardcover, elastic band; 22 × 31 × 3.5 cm (closed)
Numbered edition of 250
Courtesy of the author
(p. 99)

Carolina Caycedo (England, 1978)
*YUMA, or the Land of Friends,* 2014

Satellite images, digital prints on acrylic glass; 580 × 473 cm
Courtesy of the authors
(p. 99)

Futurefarmers (founded in 1995)
*Seed Journey,* 2016–17

Three-channel video work, prints, objects
Courtesy of the authors
Photo by Monica Løvdahl
(pp. 104–05)

Marjetica Potrč (Slovenia, 1953)
*New Territories in Acre and Why They Matter,* 2008

Text
Courtesy of the author
First published in *e-flux journal* 00, November, 2008

Erik Sjödin (Sweden, 1979)
*Our Friends the Pollinators,* 2014–ongoing

Workshop
Courtesy of the artist

**HeK + LABoral**

Joana Moll (Spain, 1982)
*CO2GLE,* 2014

JavaScript, HTML; dimensions variable
Courtesy of the artist
(p. 108)

Joana Moll (Spain, 1982)
*DEFOOOOOOOOOOOOOOOOO OOOOOREST,* 2016

JavaScript, HTML; dimensions variable
Courtesy of the artist
Acknowledgement: Ramin Soleymani
(p. 109)

Chris Jordan (USA, 1963)
*Albatross* film trailer, 2017

Video; 3 min, 49 sec
Courtesy of the artist
(p. 118)

Gilberto Esparza (Mexico, 1975)
*BioSoNot 2.0,* 2017

Microbial fuel cells, electronic circuits, polycarbonate, silicone, stainless steel, carbon fiber, aluminum, multi-parameter sensors, wastewater; 99 × 30 × 50 cm
In collaboration with Daniel Llermaly and Diego Liedo
Courtesy of the artist
(p. 111)

Marcus Maeder (Switzerland, 1971)
*treelab,* 2017

Spatial audio and stereo sound installation
Artistic realization and sonification by Marcus Maeder (ICST), scientific data and analysis by Roman Zweifel (WSL), programming support by Philippe Kocher, Thomas Peter (ICST), technical engineering field measurements by Jonas Meyer (ICST, Decentlab)
Photo by Maeder/Zweifel; courtesy of Marco Zanoni
Courtesy of the artist
(pp. 122–23)

Juanjo Palacios (Spain, 1966)
*Reserva Sonora de la Biosfera de Asturias: Mapa sonoro v 1.0,* 2018

Digital cartography
Courtesy of the artist
Acknowledgements: Asturias Tourism
(pp. 162–63)

Terike Haapoja (Finland, 1974)
*Inhale–Exhale,* 2008/13

Durational sculptures; plywood, glass, soil, CO2 sensors, sound
Programming by Aleksi Pihkanen, Gregoire Rousseau, scientific advising by Eija Juurola and Toivo Pohja
Photos by Sandra Kantanen
(pp. 106–07)

Aline Veillat (France, 1967)
*Pas de deux en vert et contre,* 2009–12

Living plants and robotic, autonomous, and interactive installation
In collaboration with Autonomous Systems Lab (ASL), ETHZ (Pr. Roland Siegwart and his team), the Department of Environmental Sciences at ETHZ (Dr. Sebastian Leuzinger), Tegoro Solutions AG, FULGURO, Lausanne
(p. 114)

Rasa Smite and Raitis Smits
(Latvia, 1969 and 1966)
*Fluctuations of Microworlds,* 2017

Generative audiovisual installation; 360-degree video, data visualization in virtual reality, time-lapse video, data sculpture, digital prints, objects
Support: State Culture Capital Foundation of Latvia, Riga City Council, the Ministry of Culture of the Republic of Latvia, Nordplus, Liepaja University, Art Research Lab of Liepaja University
(p. 117)

Anne Marie Maes (Brussels, 1955)
*Intelligent Guerilla Beehive,* 2016

High-density foam, bio-fabric, vacuum, 3D printing, electronics (solar panel, camera, Raspberry Pi, cables), biofilm with bacterial monitoring system; dimensions variable
In collaboration with Fablab Barcelona, DIYBio Barcelona, Joeri Bultheel, and JRC, Ispra
Courtesy of the artist
(p. 112)

Baggenstos/Rudolf
(Heidy Baggenstos and Andreas Rudolf, Switzerland, 1958 and 1970)
*Fostering Duckweed—From Urine to Protein,* 2016–17

Installation; dimensions variable
Courtesy of the artist
(p. 121)

**knowbotiq** (Yvonne Wilhelm and Christian Huebler, Switzerland, 1962)
*Genesis Machines: La Pompa Agricultura Transsubstantiata,* 2018

Multimedia and performative installation
In collaboration with Nicolas Buzzi (granular synthesis), Fred Hystère (molecular listening), Claudia de Serpa Soares (figurations), Angi Nend (micro surveillance), Pablo Alarcón (translucent materials)
Photos by Joachim Dette, photographed during the performance at the symposium "Unbound 1948," HKW, Berlin, 2018
Courtesy of the artists
(p. 136)

María Castellanos and Alberto Valverde (Spain, 1985 and 1967)
*Symbiotic Interaction,* 2017

Two technological body interfaces; dimensions variable
This project has been possible thanks to a residency at Softlab and Sliperiet at the Art Campus of the University of Umeå, Sweden, 2016–17
(pp. 126–27)

Ursula Biemann (Switzerland, 1955)
*Acoustic Ocean,* 2018

Video installation; 18 minutes
Design of the props by Michael Graessner, performance by Sofia Jannok, camera by Lydia Zimmermann, soundtrack by Patrick Codenys, commissioned by The Atlantic Project, Plymouth, for the exhibition *After the Future—in the Wake of Utopian Imaginaries*
(pp. 146–47)

**HeK**

**HeHe** (founded in France, 1999)
*Domestic Catastrophe N° 3: La Planète Laboratoire,* 2012

Globe, aquarium, water, engine, lightning, audio installation, timer, electronic components; dimensions variable
Courtesy of Aeroplastics Brussels, commissioned by l'Espace Fondation EDF and Cape Farewell for the exhibition *Carbone 12—Art et Changement climatique*
(pp. 166–67)

**LABoral**

**Semiconductor** (founded in UK, 1999)
*Earthworks,* 2016

Five-channel computer generated animation with four-channel surround sound
Edition of 3 + 1 AP
Photo by Sergi A. Minguell
Courtesy of Fundació Sorigué, Lleida
(pp. 28–29)

Terike Haapoja (Finland, 1974)
*Dialogue,* 2008

Interactive installation, live trees, electronics, sound, light, CO2 sensors, breathing
Programming by Aleksi Pihkanen and Gregoire Rousseau, scientific consulting by Eija Juurola and Toivo Pohja
(p. 125)

Unknown Fields Division
(founded in UK, 2008)
*Unravelled,* 2017

Video installation; dimensions variable
Textile design by Unknown Fields, produced in collaboration with Navneet Raman, film directed by Unknown Fields in collaboration with Tushar Prakash, director of photography: Ravi Kiran Ayyagari, starring: Monica Jha
In partnership with the Architectural Association
Courtesy of the artists
(pp. 128–29)

Joaquín Fargas (Argentina, 1950)
*Glaciator,* 2017

Aluminum, solar panels, GPS, mechatronics; dimensions variable
Acknowledgements: Universidad Maimónides, credits: Santiago Clancy, Elia Gasparolo
(p. 115)

This book is published in conjunction with the exhibitions:

**Eco-Visionaries**
**Art, Architecture, and New Media after the Anthropocene**

MAAT—Museu de Arte, Arquitetura e Tecnologia, Lisbon, Portugal
Eco-Visionários
April 10–October 8, 2018

Bildmuseet, Umeå, Sweden
Ekologins Visionärer
June 15–October 21, 2018

HeK—Haus der elektronischen Künste Basel, Switzerland
Eco-Visionaries
August 30–November 11, 2018

LABoral Centro de Arte y Creación Industrial, Gijón, Spain
Eco-Visionarios
Spring 2019

Editor:
Pedro Gadanho

Curators:
Pedro Gadanho
Sabine Himmelsbach
Sofia Johansson
Karin Ohlenschläger
Mariana Pestana
Yvonne Volkart

Contributing authors:
Amale Andraos
T. J. Demos
Matthew Fuller
Linda Weintraub

Managing editor:
Nuno Ferreira de Carvalho

Copyediting:
Benjamin Barlow

Graphic design and typesetting:
Julia Wagner, grafikanstalt

Typeface:
Alright sans, Scout condensed

Production:
Moana Müller, Hatje Cantz

Project management:
Juliane Eisele, Hatje Cantz

Printing and reproductions:
Longo SpA, Bolzano

Binding:
Gruppo Padovana, Padua

Paper:
Profibulk 1.1, 150 g/m²

© 2018 Hatje Cantz Verlag, Berlin, and authors

Published by
Hatje Cantz Verlag GmbH
Mommsenstraße 27
10629 Berlin
Tel. +49 30 3464678-00
Fax +49 30 3464678-29
www.hatjecantz.de
A Ganske Publishing Group Company

Hatje Cantz books are available internationally at selected bookstores. For more information about our distribution partners, please visit our website at www.hatjecantz.com.

ISBN 978-3-7757-4453-9

Printed in Italy

FSC
www.fsc.org
MIX
Paper from
responsible sources
FSC® C023164